NO ORDINARY NEIGHBOUR

NO ORDINARY NEIGHBOUR

Conversations with one of the last surviving members of Hitler's SS

BRUCE D. THOMPSON

FRONTLINE
BOOKS

First published in Great Britain in 2026
by Frontline Books
An imprint of
Pen & Sword Books Ltd
Yorkshire – Philadelphia

ISBN 9781036185886

A CIP catalogue record for this book is available from the British Library.

Typeset by Lapiz Digital
Printed and bound CPI UK

FSC
www.fsc.org
MIX
Paper | Supporting responsible forestry
FSC® C013604

The Publisher's authorised representative in the EU for product safety is Authorised Rep Compliance Ltd., Ground Floor, 71 Lower Baggot Street, Dublin D02 P593, Ireland.
www.arccompliance.com

For a complete list of Pen & Sword titles please contact
PEN & SWORD BOOKS LIMITED
47 Church Street, Barnsley, South Yorkshire, S70 2AS, England
E-mail: enquiries@pen-and-sword.co.uk
Website: www.pen-and-sword.co.uk
or
PEN AND SWORD BOOKS
1950 Lawrence Road, Havertown, PA 19083, USA
E-mail: uspen-and-sword@casematepublishers.com
Website: www.penandswordbooks.com

This book is dedicated to its readers – that, for the sake of the present and future, we may together reflect on what is told and written of the past.

Please note - excerpts from Erwin's memoirs are unaltered and all typos and grammatical errors are retained for authenticity.

CONTENTS

ACKNOWLEDGMENTS

First and foremost, I want to acknowledge all those who have shared their story with me over the years, especially the Holocaust survivors and the veterans who served. Amongst the survivors I wish to especially mention: the amazing Hanneke Dye, the irrepressible Professor Agnes Kaposi, the late Gisela Feldman who was aboard the *St Louis*, the late Jan Fuchs who fled Prague 'after Hitler came', and the late and extraordinary Eva Schloss, who became Anne Frank's posthumous stepsister following the marriage of Eva's mother Fritzi to Anne's father Otto.

My grandfather Norman served in the Royal Marines during the war and thankfully fostered my interest in the Second World War from an early age.

My primary school teacher, and later friend, Tom Pilsbury was a Normandy veteran; he connected me to a place and time that would become so much part of this story.

There were so many other British veterans that I had the enormous privilege of knowing and hearing their stories over the course of my ministry that I cannot name them all; however, they influenced me greatly and helped develop within me a better understanding of those years than any history book or TV documentary could.

My good friend the Revd Rob Blackhall, who was Chaplain at Queen's College, Taunton and who presided over the Holocaust Memorial Event that brought Erwin and I together. I will forever be grateful that Rob had the courage to host the event, not just because without that occasion Erwin and I may not have met, but because he gave the students opportunities to learn of the horrors of the Holocaust and subsequent genocides.

David Clitheroe has so often been a pillar of strength for me over many years; it was to him I turned when I first needed to unburden my feelings after the significance of my relationship with Erwin became apparent. If I were Erwin's confessor David was surely mine. There were times in my ministry when I hung on because David gave his time to me.

Digitising Erwin's photographic negatives was a key turning point in my relationship with Erwin, without them I may never have elicited from Erwin the names of those senior officers he served under. I am indebted to Paul Dowker for undertaking this sensitive task with such professionalism.

Martin Howe came to Erwin's rescue (and mine) several times when his computer needed attention or he wanted to forward a document to me.

Dr Jaswant Singh Phul spent much time with me discussing the criminal mind, the moulding of the soldier's behaviour, and the mental processing of how to live with being complicit in a terrible act. It was good to be given greater confidence in my attempts at understanding why Erwin acted as he did.

I am indebted to a lawyer with expertise in international criminal law who gave me good advice.

Dr Henry Tann, for his stalwart encouragement and interest. His enthusiasm is infectious and helped instil within me a belief in the importance of this book.

Rebecca Fairbank, for her help in researching Erwin's past, and for shedding light upon it through her experience as a historian and TV documentary producer of ancestry and military programmes.

The late Dr John Leonard who for more than thirty years nurtured my self-belief and enquiring mind. He set before me and many others an example of how to live in the service of others.

William Horwood shed light on writing from his many years as an author, not least how to let creativity flow: to write down what is on one's mind rather than be troubled at that moment whether it was in chronological order, such matters could wait till later.

Without Kathryn Marshall-Kirchberger the initial requests to the *Bundesarchiv* would have been that much more difficult to make. I am so grateful for her expertise in translating both my correspondence and some of the documents Erwin provided me with. Kathryn was also of great help in translating pages from Erwin's Soldbuch. She too, through her own enthusiasm in the project, drove me on.

Martin Mace, the Commissioning Editor at Frontline Books, was an enthusiastic supporter from the moment he read the submission. He spurred me on to complete the text with growing confidence, confirming my belief that this was a story that needed to be told.

John Grehan edited the manuscript and was most generous and kind in his analysis even if he did take out 208 semi-colons; well John, here is another that I hope you won't remove!

I recall with much appreciation the courage of the four women who participated in the event that addressed their experiences as Germans born after the war – they must remain anonymous because I have lost contact with all but one. However, should they have picked up this volume I hope they will know that they have my utmost respect.

Erwin would not have remained in his home for as long as he did, nor indeed lived so long without Judith and Andrew Bosier. They were true friends to him and gave up so much of their time and energies in ensuring he was cared for and his needs were met. They were gracious in keeping me abreast of Erwin's situation.

This account would have been somewhat different had I met Martina Böhme much earlier than Erwin's death, but the knowledge she had through a longer friendship than I was privileged to have with him meant that she was able to endorse much of that which I had come to know. She became an invaluable friend and advisor as I finalised this book. We had a shared affection and respect for Erwin, but neither of us were under any illusions as to the gravity of the actions of his unit.

Finally, I must pay tribute to my wonderful family David and Sarah, Robert and Katie, and especially my patient and sometimes not so patient, justifiably so, wife Karen. They put up with my absences over the course of my ministry as I gave my time to others; they dealt with my mood swings - my moments of enthusiasm and moments of frustration; they must have grown tired when my excitement at what I was involved with took over the room; they deserve the last word over someone who is often keen to have it.

FOREWORD

Bruce Thompson, a true pastor, a deeper listener by nature and vocation, had often sat with World War II veterans, soldiers who landed on D-Day and fought in Normandy and former allied air personnel. He had also increasingly come into contact with survivors of the Holocaust, inviting them to speak on memorial days about the horrors they went through and what their experiences had come to mean to them. He had long been aware of the grim history of Jew hatred and was frank about the role of the church and its ministers in fanning the coals of antisemitism.

What, then, is Thompson to do when, after a Holocaust Memorial Day event, he is asked a question by a polite elderly gentleman by the name of Erwin who is keen to engage with him but turns out to be a former German soldier in the Second World War? Is it appropriate for him to develop a connection with a man with such a background? Yet he is curious. As the relationship between the two men deepens from cordiality into a complex and paradoxical friendship, Thompson becomes increasingly determined to find out all he can about Erwin's past. But he needs to be patient; he soon realises that Erwin may be affable, but he is also cunning: if he wants to discover the full facts of what he did in the war, he will have to take each conversation slowly over what will prove to be more than twenty years. At the same time, he pursues his own research which quickly confirms what he had suspected from very early on: Erwin was in the SS, in the Leibstandarte Adolf Hitler no less, fighting on the Eastern Front, in Italy and in France. But what did he actually do? What did he know? What did those around him do and know?

However, it would be a mistake to read this book as a detective story about Erwin's past. The true questions preoccupying the author are whether and why it is right to engage with a man who served in the SS. What would his survivor friends say? Thompson is, of course, categorical in his absolute condemnation of the Holocaust and its perpetrators. But what if one were to be born into a society in which the great majority lauded and obeyed the Führer? What might one do if exposed to such pressures? Was it possible to know what acts one might prove capable, or incapable, of committing?

While his moral compass remains firm and clear, Thompson is not interested in passing judgment over Erwin. Rather, in publishing this deeply self-aware account of his relationship with him, he wants to make us face the question, frighteningly pertinent in our age of resurgent populism: what evils might a society enable and encourage ordinary people to perpetrate, and how do we, today, avoid reaching the point where we find ourselves subject to such temptations?

Skilfully written and with great personal insight, this is a courageous and disturbingly relevant book.

Jonathan Wittenberg, Senior Rabbi of Masorti Judaism UK

INTRODUCTION

This account is neither an apology nor an attempt at revisionism. Anyone looking for either will be disappointed. I cannot apologise on behalf of others. I believe that revisionism is utterly abhorrent when it comes to the Holocaust. The facts speak for themselves, despite the efforts of those that have sought to play down the nature of such an unprecedented catastrophe. The darkest episode in human history was of such a magnitude that we might examine it from many angles but never run out of new insights into why and how seemingly ordinary people turned on their neighbours in such unspeakable ways.

This account cannot be about forgiveness and rehabilitation, how could it be? Forgiveness is not in my gift. None of my family were victims of the Holocaust, so the impact of it upon my life has only been through sitting with survivors, hearing their stories, feeling their pain, and, having listened, had the privilege of calling them friends. I would be the last person on earth to underestimate the hurt of those who have suffered so much.

Over the course of my life, I have found that when someone not on the receiving end of actions that caused offence, hurt, or serious damage, seeks to rehabilitate a person for their misdemeanour they might only serve to inflict further wounds on those that have been harmed. Nor should anyone else, especially the victims, be expected by others to forgive those that did grievous harm to someone.

However, what I have sought to do here is provide an honest record of a relationship that lasted more than twenty years and reflect upon it as best I am able. I did not initiate the relationship, though some might argue that I could have ended it at any time; indeed, there were periods when I thought the relationship had concluded. There were times of frantic conversation and there were times of silence, long periods of silence in fact. After a while, what began as a trickle became a gushing river.

This account, then, is about patience and impatience in a relationship. It is about secrecy and openness. It is about fear and hope. It is about shame, and wrestling with the consequences of an interlocutor being an agent of an evil regime. I believe there are lessons for us all to learn here, not so much about actual events of the Second World War, these are probably better recorded elsewhere, but lessons on how someone close to those events suppressed his memories thereafter. This account is especially about how that person, a veteran of Hitler's elite SS, the Leibstandarte no less, slowly revealed his story to me, sometimes because of my gentle prompting, sometimes because of my determination to get to the truth, and sometimes because he simply wanted someone to hear what he had been carrying with him for sixty to eighty years.

We know that we are often tempted to believe only the first story we hear, or maybe the one that fits with our own perspectives and beliefs, and not the version that comes later, perhaps one that not only informs but challenges the previous. Listening to subsequent versions of the same story does not necessarily discredit the first, but it is to remember that in any engagement, in any encounter, there are at least two perspectives.

Another challenge is that many prefer to keep on endorsing a version of history that makes them feel good, perhaps of being on the side of the morally just; I have found this course of action to be unhelpful. If I only hear the side of the victim, how can I ever understand why the perpetrator acted as they did? That is in no way to be disrespectful of the victim, nor is to underestimate the pain inflicted upon them. However, if I am to learn from experience, to prevent myself from acting irresponsibly, or from being swept along by the tide of overwhelming opinion, then surely it is my responsibility to fully examine the intentions, actions, and conscience of those that became agents, or supporters, of an evil regime.

When something horrendous takes place, there are some questions we often choose not to ask, not least how did all this begin? Or what was it that made people behave in the way they did? Were some merely caught up in the zeitgeist, evil though that may have turned out to be? Did they later come to regret having been swept along? If so, where should the blame lie? In addition, what happens if an expression of regret takes place? Should it fall on deaf ears?

The honest know that evil has a habit of manifesting itself in many ways. It can even give the impression that it is the greater good, especially in the maelstrom of cataclysmic change with the future so uncertain. This has been the pattern of the centuries, and yet within each generation we must learn this brutal truth: that every human being has a capacity to both do great good and inflict great harm; often it all depends on the circumstances in which they find themselves. I guess the fundamental question for us all is: how would I have responded given the context and circumstances?

Therefore, I believe that unthinking condemnation in a later generation would be an inappropriate act. Unless we can put our hand on heart and say with conviction that, somehow, we would have been able to resist the adrenalin rush of the crowd; that we would have had the capacity to free ourselves completely of making wrong choices, we should be very wary of engaging in naïve condemnation. I am not so confident in how I might have responded given certain settings. I cannot say in all honesty that I have never made an error of judgment nor been swept along by peer pressure. Circumstances have a habit of making us who we are. The millions of decisions we make over the course of a lifetime can never be entirely free of fault. How we respond to our mistakes and the honesty with which we lead our lives, now they are other matters entirely.

Rev. Bruce Thompson,
Didcot, March 2026.

'Will compelling a dying man on that journey through the years amount to anything other than a futile confrontation with what had long vanished into history and could not be changed? Nor do I know whether the things that happened in those far-off days might be ameliorated by words uttered in the present, or if it is possible that the memory could be salved, however selfishly or too conveniently. I no longer feel able to make the judgements that I clutched securely when setting out and, as we sit in the fire's light, the sweep of history seems to unravel into nothing more than the never-ending days in which we lived. Days filled with both piety and shame which can never be fully disowned no matter how much we try.'

David Park
Spies in Canaan *(Bloomsbury Publishing, 2022)*

Chapter 1

A GLIMPSE OF WHAT WAS TO COME

One photograph stood out. Each of them was of interest and quite a few of them especially so. However, one presented the most significant piece of evidence that there was more to what Erwin had disclosed thus far. Erwin had presented an envelope to me in the autumn of 2021. He claimed that it contained the only negatives that had survived the war. There were just eight and each of them excited me. Mindful of the sensitivity of digitising and developing the negatives, I had to give a great deal of thought as to how this could be done without the images falling into the hands of others. Having wrestled with the dilemma, I recalled someone who was a lecturer in photography and who would know how to proceed. I was grateful to Paul who, without a second thought, agreed to undertake the work. When he returned with the file of images, and we sat around my computer to view them, my excitement increased.

I could now see what Erwin looked like during the war, what his comrades looked like, and from one photograph I was able to clearly locate him in a town in Northern France (Plate 1). Though the image is not perfect, with a shade across the bottom half, Erwin is seen as fresh faced and little more than a boy; there can be few other ways of describing his appearance. He looks as though he may still be at school, except he is in a heavy woollen greatcoat with Nazi military insignia on his left sleeve, together with the rank of *Sturmmann* (Lance Corporal). His fair hair is short and tidy, and maybe recently clipped. It has a parting and sweeps to the right with a wave in it. Erwin's woollen-gloved hands are clasped together at waist level, the left hand inside the right. The greatcoat is mid-calf in length and looks slightly too big for him. His highly polished jackboots can just be seen beneath the greatcoat. Erwin is posing for the photograph, his eyes looking to his left and he is standing next to the town sign of Livarot a small French town, 50km to the southeast of Caen. The sign indicates that it is on the N179. It is extraordinary to think that this photograph would have been taken during the regiment's refit in France a little while after Erwin had spent the winter of 1941-42 in Ukraine.

A second photograph captured a moment of pride for Erwin in his military service (Plate 2). He had previously recounted to me how he trained as a lorry driver in France. The image shows an older Erwin than the first image: Erwin is standing next to the front of the truck, trying to give the appearance that he is relaxed, as if the photograph is not posed in any way. He is leaning on the wheel guard and is again looking away from the lens of the camera. The number plate clearly displays the SS runes. Above the plate is another sign stating, '*Ecole de Chauffeur*', driving school. The passenger door is open and maybe the driving instructor is the one taking the photograph. Erwin's uniform carries, on his forearm, the band worn by members of the SS Leibstandarte Adolf Hitler regiment – the band is black and the name Adolf Hitler, though not clear, is emblazoned across it. What can only just be made out is a strip of material fastened to the second button of his tunic; this indicates that Erwin is a veteran of the Russia campaign. In the background are buildings and an Esso sign.

The other six photographs merely show Erwin with his comrades in small groups, all in France. In one, a group of sixteen appear to have been on some form of parade (Plate 3). One, fourth from the left, is looking very pleased with himself. There is something in his left hand, the man next to him, to his right, is looking down at it with a degree of interest, as if it is something significant; is it a medal in a case? Another is holding what looks like a scrap of paper. All appear to be wearing the Russia campaign ribbon on their tunics, one or two look exhausted. Another seems to be staring into space; I cannot help but feel that there is great fear in his empty eyes. What have these men seen? What have they done?

I was more than pleased with what I had received from Erwin and deeply grateful for the work done by Paul. For almost twenty years I had no idea what Erwin had looked like during the war, but thanks to the photographs I could now picture him clearly. I could also locate him in a specific place. The stories he had shared with me previously had now become ever more real.

Just when I had grown used to having in my possession this treasure of eight photographs, I received a phone call from Erwin. During the call, Erwin mentioned that he had discovered a few more negatives.

I was naturally keen to get hold of them as soon as I could, but could not identify in my diary a slot when I could travel. After much thought I managed to ask my friend David, who lived not far from Erwin, to collect them. David was about to attend my son and daughter-in-law's wedding, so he could hand them over to me then. This was acceptable to Erwin as he had met David before and knew that we could trust him with the negatives.

When David gave them to me, I was shocked. There were far more than eight negatives this time and they were contained in a small box. I later discovered that the box held no fewer than seventy-two negatives. I could not help but feel this to be yet another example of Erwin stringing things out. Time and again over twenty years Erwin would drip something into our conversation that would tease me into wanting more. Once I had become satisfied, something additional would be hinted at. Earlier Erwin had claimed that the cache of eight negatives was all that he had retained from the war, but now a new cache of seventy-two had suddenly appeared.

Again, I drew on the discretion and generosity of Paul who digitised and developed all the images. One photograph stood out. This photograph would change everything. It would confirm my worst suspicions. It would also add a face, and a name, that would send a chill down my spine. It added something darker to a comment Erwin had made in an unusually off-guarded moment: 'I got used to the sight of bodies; I was taught how to pack them on a lorry in such a way as to make the best use of the space.' I later discovered that the Nazis coined a phrase for their method of packing bodies in a grave following a massacre: 'sardine packing.'

However, there were more years, many more conversations, and not a little teasing on the part of Erwin, which I found frustrating but had to learn to deal with, before we were to get any confirmation that Erwin had witnessed terrible things. What did become increasingly apparent as the years advanced and my understanding grew, was how my relationship with Erwin was not only informing me of the past, but of the present too. Little did I know when I first met Erwin how much the world about us would change over the course of our twenty-year relationship.

The first decades of my twenty-first century world began to resonate with Erwin's world of the 1930s. A first-hand account of how he had been drawn into one of the most feared units in military history offered insights into how others today could effortlessly be drawn into extremist ideologies. A failure to listen and learn from this ongoing conversation would have been a dereliction of duty on my part.

PART I
ENCOUNTERS

Chapter 2

THE FIRST ENCOUNTER (2004)

'So, you're a clever man; tell me, could it have been avoided?' The question set off an acquaintanceship of many years. It would take me on a journey of fascination and discovery, shock, and horror, about the man who stood before me that day, about myself, and about the perpetrators of atrocities on the Eastern Front and elsewhere during the Second World War.

By the time of our first encounter, I had already been exposed to the devastating impact the Holocaust had inflicted on people I had come to know. I had dedicated much of my spare time over the previous few years to hastily catching up on seeking to understand the events that made up one of the worst crimes in human history. It had only been four years since I had begun sitting in on events where survivors gave accounts of life in the ghettoes, of transports, death camps, forced marches, and liberation. I had only just begun the long and painful attempt to understand why it was that the German churches had appeared to fail in their response to Nazi antisemitism.

It is difficult for me to identify when I first became aware of the Holocaust. There may not have been a single, defining moment, but, more likely, a gradual disclosure of one of the vilest acts of mass murder the planet has known. Whilst I did not watch the TV drama *Holocaust*, knowledge of its broadcast in 1978, and the occasional trailer, triggered something in my mind. It was a fictional account of two German families, one Jewish, the Weiss family, the other Aryan, the Dorf family. I would later discover that the series was heavily criticised by leading survivors and academics, but it had raised in my teenage consciousness an awareness of the darkest chapter of the Second World War that, up till then, had not been properly considered in my hearing. Instead, my mind had been focussed on Dunkirk, D-Day, the Arctic and North Atlantic convoys, Pearl Harbor and Hiroshima.

Auschwitz, Birkenau, Bergen-Belsen, Buchenwald, Dachau and Theresienstadt would have been places beyond my vocabulary, let alone understanding, at the time.

There seems little reason why a working-class boy growing up in a mono-cultural south Staffordshire coal-mining town in the 1960s and '70s should have been exposed to stories of such places of atrocity. Methodist Sunday School had taught me that 'the Jews' had gone from shouting 'Hosanna' on Palm Sunday to 'Crucify' on Good Friday, teaching that I later learnt had helped fuel hostility toward Jews over centuries.

In addition, to my young mind, the war had been about stopping Hitler invading Britain, little else. Often as a child, I would hear adults say to one another that had we have 'lost the war we'd all be talking German by now'. That seemed an odd thing to me. I began to wonder what life could have been like had we lost the war; what it would be like to be speaking a wholly different language. In my naïve infantile mind, I dared to suggest that that would be interesting, to which I was roundly informed 'I doubt you would have even been born'.

That disturbed me; not being born was beyond my comprehension. I could not even begin to imagine not having a consciousness, to have remained in a perpetual state of unknowing, of not being. Weird. Moreover, shocking. Yet, I was growing up in a household of grief – I had been conceived just two months before my father suddenly died at 23. His mother raised me for the four years until her death in 1963. My own mother married a widower with four children. The thought of not being born, of not existing, was disturbing to say the least. Therefore, the Nazis had a lot to answer for, and my gratitude to my grandfathers' generation for fighting off this terrible threat grew immeasurably. I owed my very existence to the sacrifice of those men and women four or five decades my senior.

Nevertheless, I also grew up close to the German Military Cemetery on Cannock Chase, Staffordshire. It is estimated that between 5 and 6,000 German military personnel died in the UK during the two world wars; nearly 5,000 Germans, Austrians, and a few Ukrainians had been re-interred there, and I can recall its opening in June 1967 shortly before my eighth birthday. Indeed, I can also recall my grandfather, who had served in the Royal Marines in the Second World War, taking me along one evening to observe the day's work through the fence as graves were freshly dug and filled. Incidentally, the agreement between the British and West German governments to create this imposing and mournful site had been made just two weeks after my birth in 1959. As a child and teenager, I often wandered amongst the graves, reading names and thinking about the grief of their families on hearing that a loved one had died. Even if they had been members of forces bent on destroying the UK, they were still, to my young mind, human beings with stories to tell, if only they could. Looking back, I have no doubt now that this experience lay the groundwork for what was to come many years later, making me open and receptive to a story that could still be told.

However, what the Nazis and their accomplices had done to Jewish communities, in far off and mysterious places on the continent of Europe, was yet to be revealed to me. As an eighteen-year-old, when I caught that first glimpse of a trailer for the TV series *Holocaust*, it featured whole families, with yellow stars sewn on to their coats, crowded together on a platform being herded into cattle trucks. It was night, there was steam from the locomotive, they were wearing hats, and there was panic on their faces. At least that is how I remember it. It became a recurring memory for me. I wanted to know more; over time I did learn more.

That said, it was not until twenty years later that I would sit in a synagogue and hear a first-hand account from someone who had been on a real platform, had worn a real yellow star, had been herded onto a real cattle truck, and spoke of smelling roasted human flesh on arrival at a death camp. To hear his account was shocking. To be in his presence was humbling. I knew then that I had to do something.

At that point I was seven years into my second appointment as a church minister and was well established there, so it was not difficult for me to begin sharing with members my increasing awareness of the Holocaust. They were sympathetic and understood my growing desire to know more of what had taken place six decades earlier. There were many reasons for this, not least that we were living in an area of Manchester where it was possible to encounter survivors or their children; they were our neighbours, our colleagues, our friends.

Nevertheless, I was not to remain in Manchester for long. Three years later, in 2002, I moved to the West Country. It was there that the question was posed, 'Could it have been avoided?'

When I moved to Somerset to begin a new role in the Church, I took with me an enthusiasm to raise further awareness of the lessons we could draw from those dark days of six decades before. My friend, now the late Rabbi Brian Fox of Manchester, where I had lived for much of my adult life, had charged me with building a synagogue in Taunton, a somewhat tall order for a Methodist minister! What was within my range, however, was to help my congregations and the wider community to recognise our own prejudices which, unless we check them early, could lead to further offence and injury.

At the time of my relocation the British National Party was gaining votes in local elections, and the rise of the far-right was troubling me. I felt it my duty to do what I could to challenge the warped and dangerous mind-set that was beginning to show itself in the mainstream of British politics; even a member of my congregation had expressed sympathy for those living next door to someone from overseas: 'It's not very nice, you know.' The local newspaper was warning its readers of plans to create a centre for asylum seekers in the area, which only served to whip up more hostility. This was just a microcosm of what was happening across Britain. All I could do was seek to resist such growing resentment in my own context. Part of that response was to encourage learning of faiths other than our own, which included a Judaism Awareness month followed by an Islam Awareness month, with speakers from each faith addressing religious, cultural, and political issues. All this in an area where there was no physical centre for any religious community other than Christian; even the largest group, the growing Muslim community, hired the local YMCA for Friday prayers, festivals, and the occasional celebration.

It was in this setting that the Chaplain of the local independent Methodist School, Revd. Rob Blackhall, and I organised a Holocaust Memorial Day event in the main hall of the school. The occasion would be open to the public. It was at the end of the event that the question was put to me: 'Could it have been avoided?'

The man who stood before me was tall, silver-haired, distinguished looking, bespectacled, and wearing a black leather, three-quarter length jacket, check shirt, sharply creased trousers, and highly polished shoes. His presence was not quite intimidating, but still resolute and firm. He was straight-backed, my height, if not a fraction taller, or at least he seemed to be; maybe his manner gave me that impression. He looked me in the eye. His eyes were sharp and crystal blue. His lips clenched tight below his neatly trimmed moustache. His voice soft and inviting, not judgmental but serious. His accent non-descript, if anything a touch of Welsh. Dozens of students must have been leaving the auditorium and chatting as they passed us, but I was oblivious to them. I had no idea where this man was coming from, even though I had greeted him earlier, before the event had even begun.

The event was set to commence at 11.30 hours. I arrived forty minutes early and was surprised to find a couple seated at the end of the third row in the centre aisle. The Queen's Hall, which could seat

400, was otherwise unoccupied. As I walked down the aisle towards the stage, I naturally stopped and offered a welcoming handshake. I thought little of their early arrival as they told me they had seen the event advertised and wanted to be there; maybe they had travelled a distance, maybe they were unfamiliar with the layout of the school and had misjudged how long it would take to get there? I could not say, nor did a reason seem to be of importance.

Few others would join them in the audience for quite some time, but when the event got underway there were around 400 students from the school and 75 from the wider community in attendance. It was standing room only. I can no longer recall much of the event itself. What I can remember is my friend and colleague, the school's Chaplain Rob, walking up and down the side aisles pointing to posters produced by Beth Shalom, the National Holocaust Museum and Centre near Newark in Nottinghamshire. These featured images from both the Holocaust and subsequent genocides, Cambodia, Rwanda etc. In large letters on each poster was the word *'Why?'* Rob went to each poster in turn and shouted out the question. Nothing more. Just pointed to the word and asked the question that should be on all our lips: Why?

It was only the fourth year that Britain had commemorated a National Holocaust Memorial Day. At that time, the horrors of the Holocaust were only just beginning to slip from memory to history, and it was only recently that the subject had been placed on the school curriculum. To me, it felt progressive to hold a Holocaust Commemoration in Taunton. In subsequent years the event would move to a town centre Anglican Church and be organised in partnership with the County Council, with large numbers of staff taking an extended lunch break to attend. Survivors would address us, and out of those precious occasions, a small Jewish community would come together and form a social and cultural group, not quite the synagogue I had been charged to build by my old friend Rabbi Fox, but a significant outcome, nonetheless.

However, on that cold January morning in 2004, in a well-heated school auditorium, sat a man who had a story to tell. How much he was prepared to share at that moment, or at any point later, remains uncertain to me to this day. Neither of us could have known that this was the beginning of an extraordinary relationship through which the story would eventually unfold. Nevertheless, he began with a statement and a question: 'So, you're a clever man, tell me, could it have been avoided?'

I was not sure where he was coming from. Who could have known? As I said, his voice betrayed little accent, his age was impossible to discern; he could easily have been late sixties, too young to be a survivor or veteran. What had brought him to the event? What was it that caused him to rise from his seat as I passed him to leave the auditorium and follow me up the central aisle? After all, there had been almost 500 in attendance, and he had been on the third row. Yet as soon as I had arrived in the foyer and turned round to face the auditorium door through which I had passed, he was standing there before me, almost imploring me to engage. He was not agitated, but he was intent to be the first to speak to me.

Wanting to do justice to the question he had posed, I told him that it demanded a comprehensive response. I was prepared to believe that had Britain lost the First World War and faced the subsequent economic deprivation that Germany had experienced, the ball being on the other foot, as it were, then it could have happened here. I mentioned that a few years earlier, I had heard someone who had experienced Berlin in the 1930s say that it had all been allowed to take place because it was implemented step by step. I did not mention that the person sharing this opinion was a young Jewish boy put on a train by his parents and sent to England on the *Kindertransport* just a few months before the outbreak of war.

'Good answer,' the man before me nodded. 'Here is my card. Call me. Let's have a coffee and chat some more.' The man shook my hand with a firm grip. The woman at his side, half a step back until now, moved forward, reached out with her hand, and nodded. I looked at the name on the card. 'Erwin Stahlberg?' I read out. 'Yes, I was born in Berlin in 1922.'

With that, they left through the door to my right. It was only then that I noticed others were gathering around me to speak; I remember nothing of what they had to say, except the Chaplain who came over after everyone had left and said, 'You looked as though you were in a deep conversation earlier. What was all that about?' What indeed was it about?

Little could I have realised in that moment that the conversation Erwin and I had begun would continue for more than twenty years and bring me to just one step away from those aspects of the war that I could only have read about before.

Chapter 3

WELSH CAKES AND CORNED BEEF

Anne emerged from the kitchen not just with the promised cups of tea on a tray she was carrying but with a plate of Welsh cakes as well. She was an imposing figure herself, tall, strong, and resolute. Her warm smile was evident, but even at that point I could detect something else. Her eyes were focussed and fixed, they did not wander around the room; they had no reason to, it appeared to me that she and Erwin had lived in their bungalow for some years, though I was to later discover far less than I had thought at that time. Everything, packed in though it was, had its place; Anne gave me the impression that she was the sort of person who would know where every single item was, even with her eyes closed. However, for now, her eyes were wide open and asking questions of me. She had heard me address the Holocaust Memorial Day event and she had listened in during the brief conversation between her husband and I in the foyer as they were about to leave that day. But she was radiating a concern that made me slightly uncomfortable. All of this, I later came to realise, was a form of protective love. She was uneasy about what others might come to know. Not being German herself probably meant that she had likely experienced a degree of suspicion, if not prejudice and hostility, over the years because of marrying a German veteran from the Second World War. She probably had every right to be concerned and protective though, by how much, remained to be seen. But for now, all I knew was that Erwin wanted to talk.

When I had telephoned him two weeks after the Holocaust Memorial Day event Erwin did not sound at all surprised; it was as if he had been expecting the call. There was nothing to suggest he was disappointed at a slight delay in me taking up his offer to meet or taken aback at what may have been, to some, the haste in which I had responded. It was neither too late nor too soon to ring; it was the right time and I suspected then, as I do even more so today, that he had come to believe that everything has its moment. This was to be the beginning of a lengthy, yet faltering, conversation over the next twenty plus years. The call was brief; there was an instant recognition of who I was, the date was set, the address given, and nothing more needed to be said.

Erwin and Anne lived in a neighbouring town to the one where the Holocaust Memorial Day event had taken place. This intrigued me; it meant they had made a real effort to be at the school; they did not live on its doorstep. It was not far for them to travel, but far enough to suggest that they, or at least one of them, had very much wanted to be there that day. When I steadily drove into the quiet cul-de-sac, manicured lawns, bungalows for the recently retired, and flower beds awaiting the spring, I calculated the number of the house I was looking for by adding each up ahead of me. When I worked out which it was, I smiled at the Volkswagen Golf on the drive, shining in the winter sun. Despite my attempts not to think in a stereotypical manner, it just seemed a natural choice for Erwin, the famed German efficiency and allegiance and all that. Later, I was to discover that Erwin had been captured in 1944 while driving a *Kübelwagen*, 'the bucket seat car'. This was a military version of the prototype that was intended to be Hitler's 'people's car' for two adults and three children before the war, built by Volkswagen. The initial production line was halted by the outbreak of war and the *Kübelwagen* was created instead. The saloon version finally went on the market in December 1945 and was nicknamed the Beetle two decades later. It was to be a forerunner of the Volkswagen Golf that now sat on Erwin's drive.

The door was opened very soon after I had rung the bell, without much time for me to gather my thoughts. Both Erwin and Anne stood behind it in their compact hall; there was very little room for anyone else. I was ushered in to the lounge on the left. I took the seat nearest the door, with my back to it, and Erwin sat to my right. The chairs were not the type you sink into and then find it difficult to stay awake, but years of usage made them reassuringly comfortable. Anne stood next to Erwin on his left-hand side, between me and her husband. I suspected that I was in her chair, but it had been the one which Erwin's hand had indicated I was to sit in. Within seconds I had agreed to a hot drink, but Anne only departed some minutes later. When she did leave to go into the kitchen, she was not gone long – the kettle had clearly been boiled in advance of my arrival, I had been on time, and she was prepared for me to be so.

Over the next hour Erwin wanted to know as much about me as I did of him. The first thing he wanted me to hear was that he believed me to be correct when I had suggested that 'it' could have only occurred because everything was taken 'step by step.' Erwin recounted an experience from his childhood shortly before the 1933 election that took Hitler to power. I was now reminded that Erwin was older than I had initially thought, born in 1922, the man before me was already in his 80s then. The following is an extract from the memoirs he later presented to me, capturing the same incident.

> There was talk at election time about a man referred to as a 'beer hall agitator,' a rank outsider who attempted to win support by appealing to the passion of the mob. The name Hitler was mentioned more and more as the next leader of Germany. From the reputation that surrounded him, he was not at all a popular candidate. When I was 11 years old, playing in the street one day, I overheard a conversation from a couple passing, and the woman said, 'If Hitler comes to power, we might as well be buried alive.' This really frightened me and I ran home to my mother. When I told her what I had heard, she could see that I was very upset. I said that I didn't want to be buried alive, she explained to me not to take it too seriously, and I calmed down. But this remarkable statement kept coming back into my mind from time to time and certainly made me think.

Erwin's penetrating eyes had transported both him and me back to the streets of his native city, Berlin, and to the moment Hitler had come to power.

'For days I was terrified. What would happen to us? Was the old woman right? But then the flags appeared hanging from windows, bright red against grey walls; flowers bloomed in balconies, the city was filled with colour; the streets were clean and people went about their days with a spring in their step. Everything seemed so much better.'

Again, from his memoirs:

> I was still at school when Hitler became Chancellor, and believe it or not, there were many people who actually drooled over him, and viewed him as the Messiah. What became quite obvious to me was the sudden change that started to happen quite quickly. The drop in unemployment was the first to be noticed. Road works started, motorways were built all over Germany. Would you say that is good or bad? It seems that Hitler

> knew exactly what he was doing in all this. It made rapid troop transport possible. He also made the factory owners clean up the place, paint the walls, clean the windows, put flowers out, how can you say that this is all bad? But we also found out very quickly, that if you wanted to progress in any way, you needed to conform.

Erwin went on to say that he had been called up at eighteen, by which time the war between Germany and Great Britain was well underway. Having asked him where he had served, he quickly mentioned, as if in passing, the Eastern Front, before swiftly moving on to tell me that he had been captured by Americans in Brussels in 1944. He was then transferred to a holding camp in northern France guarded by British soldiers. He said the conditions were 'terrible', with little sanitation, no shelter, poor rations, and many prisoners died. This became a recurring theme in our subsequent conversations, and he had taken an almost obsessive view of the conditions in which he and his comrades were held. It was something, he said, to which the accounts in history did not refer. After some time, he was sent to PoW camps where he spent the next four years. The four years were, in his mind, a travesty. The war had been over for three years before he was released. He sternly pointed out that this was in complete contravention of the Geneva Convention. I do not think he was aware of my underlying scepticism and limited sympathy at this grievance. I believe he was too focused on his deep-seated anger at being treated, in his mind, so inhumanely for him to notice my discomfort. I certainly felt that it was an attempt on his part to get me to relate to his own sense of injustice. However, I did not want to challenge him at this point. I was prepared to play a long game. Having had my interest piqued by Erwin's mention of the Eastern Front, I wanted to know more. Nevertheless, this was not the occasion to ask too many questions. Anne had not taken her eyes off me all the time Erwin had talked, and I thought too great an interest or suspicion on my part might have closed any further conversation down.

Therefore, I changed the subject and asked about his interests. Erwin's tone improved, his face lighting up as he spoke of his love of clock making. He pointed to one on the sideboard that he had built some years previously. He was an engineer. He enjoyed working with his hands. He relished finding out how things work and mending them when broken. He was clearly a resourceful man, which was to be further confirmed on subsequent visits when his trust in me grew.

Talking about clocks led Erwin back to the war years and his captivity. He recounted an incident that would tell me so much about his character, his resourcefulness, his ability to survive, and the lengths he would go in manipulating someone for his own gain. The location was Northern France, Erwin was with hundreds if not several thousand fellow PoWs, the conditions, as noted previously, were challenging. Again, the incident was recorded in the memoirs he was to later share with me.

> It had been some time since I'd had something to eat, and that was giving me some concern. Just before noon, soldiers came into the camp and ushered everyone to one side of the field dividing the field into two halves. The reason for this became apparent when a number of trucks were driven onto the field to be placed equal distance apart in the middle of the field, and we were directed to form a queue at each truck station. When the distribution of food started, it was one packet of biscuits each and a tin of corned beef between six of us. What you must understand now is that we were all strangers to one another, and when one of us was given the tin of corned beef the soldier counted 1 to 6 and off the six of us would go. Now if you do not stick to the one with the tin and made sure it was divided into six parts, you had only your biscuits to eat. After the trucks left the field, a water tanker was brought on and drinking water was distributed. I do not want to be too judgmental, but I have seen animals at the water hole better behaved than our lot. How can you have a drink if you have no drinking vessel? I waited until someone would lend me his cup so I could have a drink. This sort of situation made you realise the predicament you were in, the survival instinct takes over, and, together with prayer, you would adjust to the conditions.
>
> I realised quite quickly that if you needed something it would have to come from the outside. I observed that occasionally a soldier would take some of us out to do some work. That made me hang around the entrance gate, looking for a chance to be selected; but what are you looking for on the outside? Well, you are on an open field day and night; there is no cover, no blanket, no drinking vessel, and no paper. When I was chosen together with some others to do some work outside I was looking for an empty tin can, some old newspapers and perhaps a cardboard box to sit on. Looking back on all of this, we were very fortunate that the weather was dry and there was no rain, although the nights were pretty cold. Those very primitive conditions made me realise how much the human body can endure. Day after day in the same clothes, not even your shoes could be taken off. There was no water, no soap, nor towel to refresh, and the toilet facilities were too diabolical to describe. From day-to-day, all you could think of was food and when the trucks came, we formed the queue automatically. That is when I remembered that I had a silver pocket watch that needed to be wound with a key. The need for food was greater than to know the time. So I decided to part with the pocket watch for food. The opportunity came at the end of one food distribution session when I approached one of the soldiers and showed

> him the watch. He was more than interested and we started bartering. I pointed to the tins of corned beef and showed seven fingers, he nodded. So we arranged a meeting by the gate after dark when the time came for the handover, he was equally careful not to be seen by his pals, and so was I. By that time I had found some companions to share my riches with, and for once the constant feeling of hunger was, if only temporarily satisfied. What the buyer did not know was that in order to wind the watch he needed the key. Would he remember what I looked like, and how would he find me on a field of 1,000 similar looking prisoners? I did not have to wait long, because the next morning I spotted him near the gate, stretching his neck looking for me. When he spotted me and knew that I had seen him he made the motion of winding, and I knew he wanted the key! When I approached him and showed him the key he was ready to take it but I motioned more food, this time biscuits. He understood and I realised that he was prepared to go and get some. Now I knew that he wasn't going to the supermarket to buy them but that was none of my concern. The handover was as clandestine as before, and I gave him the key and the deal was complete.

I could not help but smile. But it was a measured smile, and my subdued laugh was tempered by a slight concern at how wily Erwin evidently was. He had not survived the years of war by luck alone. Calculated deceit was undoubtedly a strategy he had probably drawn on over many years and in a good number of places. Over the coming years, this incident would be the benchmark by which I would measure most of our conversations. It would sometimes temper my willingness to play his game, not wanting to be the one conned into giving him more than I wanted or needed to. It acted as a reminder that even when I was engaged in an exchange of information, Erwin liked to control the dialogue. He would always seem to hold something back for another day, thus ensuring my interest and that I would return to his home.

After recounting this extraordinary incident as a PoW in Northern France Erwin fell silent, this second snippet was clearly all that I would hear that day of his wartime experiences. So, I asked how he and Anne met. This helped prolong the conversation and to lay down the foundations of potential trust.

I discovered they had met in Wales, where his final PoW camp was, after his release and later married; though this relationship held more secrets than I could ever have imagined at this stage. It certainly explained Erwin's accent, because there were times when I thought his accent was closer to Welsh than German and, indeed, Anne's closer to German than Welsh! This was a clear indication of the time they had spent in each other's company. Erwin informed me that they did not have children. For a while they had lived in the US but it had not worked out so they returned to the UK and set up home, firstly on the south coast and then in the southwest. It was only much later that I was to discover the extraordinary number of moves Erwin had undertaken over the course of the previous fifty-six years since his release from a PoW camp.

What Erwin was keen for me to hear before I departed the home was that the 'Lord' had saved him. He had always prayed and read his Bible. He had kept his Bible with him throughout the war and since. He read it every day. It now sat on the table next to his chair and its worn condition clearly highlighted that it was indeed well used. In his view, the Lord had protected him and kept him safe from harm. Church meant much to him. He and Anne had always attended church wherever they lived. These were his parting comments.

My head was spinning as I drove home. I had not held a conversation before with a German veteran of the Second World War. My mind was wondering how right all this was. I had committed myself to hearing and retelling the stories of Holocaust survivors as a means of ensuring that a rising generation would not have the excuse of ignorance about the darkest episode in human history. My allegiance would be to them, no matter what I heard from 'the other side'.

'You will come again?' Erwin had asked as he and Anne led me to the door, all smiles. He knew what the answer was. He had done enough to ensure I wanted to know more about him, about his experiences and anything he could tell me about the German perspective. He had metaphorically handed over his watch; the key would have to wait for another day.

Chapter 4

THE LONG HAUL

I was a little more deflated on leaving the house a second time. Erwin seemed somewhat reluctant to share anything in addition to what he had during my first visit. Maybe the gap between the first and second visit was too little and appeared pushy to him, I cannot say. Maybe it had seemed indecent to Erwin, another reason for the lack of candour on his part. Yet it had been Erwin, after all, who had been keen for us to meet up again. On the other hand, Anne appeared more at ease on that second visit. I wanted to think that she had grown to like me a little during my first visit. However, I suspect that due to Erwin's openness on that previous occasion she may have reined him in for my second visit, preventing him from saying much more to someone they did not really know. Maybe this was why Anne seemed more relaxed about my presence in her home and took longer in the kitchen to bring out the drinks and biscuits; she did not need to keep an ear on what Erwin may have been saying to me. She enthusiastically enquired about my family, me, and about the role I exercised in the life of the church.

Whatever the reasons were for the somewhat platitudinal conversation on that second visit I felt less enthusiastic about calling on Erwin and Anne a third time. Additionally, as I drove home, I began to wonder what on earth I was doing. Was my interest in Erwin honourable? Did I morbidly want to be close to someone who may have witnessed or even taken part in the worst crime in history? Was I engaged in something I was yet to properly understand and maybe even come to regret it? Was I being disloyal to those whom I had met who had survived camps, *Kinderstransport*,[i] and the *St Louis*[ii]? All these questions and many more only served to encourage me to back off and leave things well alone for a while.

Some months later Erwin rang and invited me to his home for a third visit. On this occasion, Erwin again mentioned the 'mistreatment' he and his comrades experienced both during their time in the holding camp in northern France and PoW camps in Britain. To move him away from his anger about captivity, I enquired about any surviving family in Germany. They had been 'on the wrong side of the line' – East Germany – when the country was divided up between the Allies. This was one of the reasons why, Erwin said, he had not returned. There was nothing, after all, to go back to and in his mind the treatment of German veterans was appalling. It was only some years later did I suspect that he may have been afraid to return to a communist-controlled state under Soviet influence, lest his service on the Eastern Front be investigated. He had a brother whom he had visited in East Germany after the wall went up. Erwin had taken western currency with him to help the family. Erwin employed the same scowl to describe his feelings about the communist regime as he had used to relay the conditions in the holding camp in northern France in the autumn of 1944. By the time the Wall had come down in 1989 Erwin had retired. He and his brother were more freely able to converse. Now it was his brother's turn to come to Erwin's assistance. On hearing how tough his and Anne's situation had become after retirement, the brother asked if Erwin was claiming his pension from the German Government. This had surprised Erwin. A pension? From what little time he had worked prior to being called up? Yes, and including his military service during the war. This had surprised Erwin. He had no idea that a military veteran was due any pension. He took great delight in telling me what had happened next.

Erwin had been captured in Brussels in September 1944. He was driving a vehicle, which I later discovered to be a *Kübelwagen*. He was carrying 'stash' or 'booty' for an officer when he spotted American soldiers. He tried to shake them off, but turned into a road that went nowhere, bringing his war to an end. Again, his memoirs that I received much later recounted the incident in greater detail:

> I received the order to prepare for a trip to Brussels, which was quite a long way from our present position. It was obvious to me that we would not be back that night. My main concern was where we would find a place to sleep when the major came to check that I was ready to go. We set off on this trip to the unknown, as far as I was concerned. I found him to be chattier than usual explaining to me the real reason for the trip. That was the first time that I heard the word 'collaborator', which now explains a lot to me. How and where he had arranged to

meet with the collaborator I do not know, but the main reason was to contact the garages that we had commandeered to let us use the heavy lifting gear for the larger vehicles that needed repair. Somehow, the major contacted our unit to send 20 drivers to collect as many vehicles as possible and drive them to safety wherever that may be. As the time went on, I was still wondering where we would spend the night, when I was directed back to the place where we had originally made contact with the collaborator. We were taken to a nice place where some very friendly people directed us to the rooms where we spent a very comfortable night's sleep.

I must assume that the major had already made plans as to what else we had to do. After a very nice breakfast we were on our way again when we were stopped by a car and the officers directed the major to the main depot. They informed the major that this depot supplied the troops with food and clothing and had been deserted by its staff. Everybody was helping themselves to everything, and they concluded 'you might as well join them'. We soon found the depot and I asked the major what to look for, and he just said cigars, cigarettes, any tinned food and whatever you think we can use. In order to make the load secure I had to put the top on the car. Boxes after boxes were stuffed into every space including the passenger seat; little did I know that this was to save my life, as the major would ride on the right front wing. When the last box was securely found a space, we made our way back to where we had made contact with the collaborator. I was parked by the roadside, when a civilian couple asked me if I could confirm the news that the British troops were in Brussels, which I was not able to confirm, and they went on their way.

At this point I must explain something which may not be known to everyone. The fuel tank of a Kűbelwagen is at the front just behind the dashboard. On the passenger side near the foot well is a glass filter, presumably to collect any condensation of water, which should regularly be dismantled and emptied. Normally there is no danger that a passenger's feet could make contact with the filter, but on this occasion, there was no space for any passenger. What happened next surprised me; Belgian flags appeared in almost every window. I rushed to the major and told him that we had better get out of here fast or it would be too late. He came out of the building with a woman and said, 'She is coming with us.' I told him that there was no room for a passenger because every space was filled with boxes. He told me to make room and the woman moved as much as possible. I was sitting in the driver's seat and had no opportunity to help. I was only concerned to get away as fast as I could. She finally got in and we set off.

Unknown to me she had forced her feet forward and in doing so broke off the filter. It was only when she said, 'There is some water running onto my feet,' that I realised what had happened. I took a cigarette packet

> from my pocket, emptied it, twisted it to a tight cone, and screwed it into the hole, which stopped the flow of fuel, all of this whilst I was still driving. Then in the distance, I saw a tank turning his gun tower to aim at me. I turned sharp left into a side street, which dislodged the major, but he did not injure himself. When I stopped the woman had just disappeared.
>
> While I was contemplating the next move, I saw a car and I signalled for it to come toward us, which he did promptly. After telling the driver my problem we attached a towrope to my car and off we went to escape to safety, or so we thought. After some distance I spotted two strange vehicles that were covered with large white cloth that had a red circle, obviously not any of our lot. Suddenly both of them opened fire with their machine guns. This brought both cars to a sudden stop and most of the occupants were killed. I considered killing myself because I had some small arms at my side but for reasons I do not know I was prevented from doing so.
>
> Both vehicles started their engines and drove past; again they fired their guns at me without any bullet hitting me. Under such circumstances your mind does not function normally. I was figuring out how I could escape being captured when a male approached and asked "Are you dead?" When I said "No" he said, 'For you the war is over.' I told him that I had a compass and would try to get back to my unit. He then explained to me 'You will not get far. You had better come with me.' The only other survivor of the attack was the driver of the car that was towing me. We were taken to a private house that must have belonged to a local official, which was acting as a collecting point. The day was the 3rd of September 1944, late afternoon, and I have no recollection of how and where I spent that first night in captivity. I was confused, and felt humiliated. These were just some of the emotions that were going through my head. I was also upset by the loss of life I had just witnessed and distressed at the uncertain future that was to follow.

As he sat before me recounting this incident, Erwin reached his left hand over to the right collar of his shirt and informed me that as soon as he had realised he was about to face his captors he had immediately ripped the insignia from his lapel. My growing interest was stimulated further. At that moment I was not quite sure if he knew I would recognise the seriousness of what he was declaring. Later I came to think it may have been another of his games, teasing me into having a greater interest. Whatever Erwin's intention was in sharing this detail of his story, the action on that day seventy years previously was an attempt to eradicate evidence of the branch of military to which he belonged. Only the SS would be concerned to remove their infamous badge from their uniform on capture, with the SS runes being on the right collar of the tunic, just as Erwin had indicated. Their notoriety would have given them a cause for alarm should they fall into the hands of the enemy. Perhaps this is why he had considered committing suicide the instant he understood he was about to be captured.

Fortunately for Erwin this was not the Soviets that had taken him prisoner but the US Army, and it was still a few months before the Waffen SS were to massacre captured US troops in the Ardennes forest. However, there had been little quarter given at the Battle of Caen in the summer of 1944, at which I later discovered Erwin had been.

Erwin continued to recall his fascinating experience of capture. Again, the memoirs are worth quoting even though not every detail within them was included in his oral testimony that afternoon of my third visit.

> The second night was spent in a large jail in Brussels. Five of us were led to a cell that had straw filled palliasses (thin straw-filled mattresses) on the floor. Before preparing to settle down to sleep, I remembered the instruction received during military training: when captured you should only give your name, rank, and number. That prompted me to remove all external identification from my uniform and together with my pay book, which contained all sorts of important information, and stuff the whole lot deep into the palliasse. My reasoning being that when the palliasse reached the end of its usefulness it would be burnt with all its contents. How wrong I was as I was to find out more than four decades later.

After the fall of the Berlin Wall and Erwin had retired, his brother suggested he write to the German ministry responsible for pensions and inform them of his serial number in the military. Erwin was dubious but he duly wrote, though I later suspected part of his reluctance was that whoever checked his claim would become aware of his unit. A mere fortnight later, much to Erwin's astonishment, he received a letter from the ministry informing him of his pension entitlement. The calculation had taken account of both his early employment and his time in the military.

To add to Erwin's amazement, included in the correspondence was a photocopy of the pay book, his *soldbuch*, he had last seen in a Belgian police cell in 1944. Someone must have not only found it but had handed it in. It was then passed on to the appropriate authorities and stored somewhere for future reference. At this moment in describing the *soldbuch* Erwin shared his dismay that at some point in its travels someone had allowed the corner of his *soldbuch* to become bent. 'I had kept that pay book in perfect condition throughout my time,' Erwin concluded. Erwin was seriously offended; however, I could not help but laugh. Someone was to later inform me that bending the corner is still a German practice of declaring a document to no longer be valid, so I may have misunderstood Erwin's alarm.

Around the living room of Erwin and Anne's small bungalow were examples of organisation. Everything had its place. I felt that if someone had asked where an item was, an item that Erwin had not touched for a while, he would be able to reach for it without hesitation. I do not think this was my own stereotyping at play, what we would now term unconscious bias, I honestly believe it was a fair analysis of the man before me. Which is why his careful analysis of what he would share and when, was to tell me something about him. I would have to wait some time for Erwin to be ready to tell me more. He knew what he was doing. As the years passed, I grew more convinced that he was aware of my own understanding of what he was doing. We were engaged in a transaction akin to the one between Erwin and the young Tommy in northern France six decades before, the latter exchanging corned beef for a pocket watch only to desperately return the next day looking for Erwin and the key to wind up the now wound down watch. He and I were still at the watch and corned beef stage, for now the key and biscuits would have to wait.

Erwin was not only meticulous both in his appearance and in his tidy, organised home, and not only was he a careful, wily character, he was also a man of great humour. He took great delight in telling me that after his and Anne's failed attempt to make a go of it in the US they had returned to the UK. Having arrived on the south coast Erwin and Anne attended a church on the first Sunday after. This was the manner of doing things for Erwin – it was important to him, to identify and attend a church as soon as he was able after moving to a new place. On this occasion it happened to be the Harvest Festival. Erwin informed me that the congregation was very pleasant. So much so that following the service, as he and Anne were about to leave, they were told that there would be a Harvest lunch once everyone had gathered in the hall and that they would be very welcome to join them. Erwin and Anne accepted the kind invitation. They sat down at a table and the other seats soon filled. The person leading worship that day was a guest preacher, an ex-minister of the congregation, Erwin believed. He was late coming into the hall as he was bidding farewell to those who could not stay for lunch. By the time he had done so there seemed to be only one seat left vacant and that seat was next to Erwin. Over lunch they exchanged pleasantries. Eventually the minister suggested that he and Erwin might be roughly the same age, so he enquired as to where Erwin was in the war. Knowing that Erwin's accent sounded a little indistinct, more Welsh than German, with perhaps a smattering of American having just returned to the UK, I can just imagine how innocent that question would have been for the minister. By way of an answer, Erwin said that for a while he served in Normandy. 'So did I', replied the minister, 'Whereabouts?' Erwin gave a wry smile as he recounted for me his response; he quickly named three towns or villages for the minister. The minister was astonished. 'Really? That is amazing. I was there too. We might have been there together.' 'No, I don't think so,' replied Erwin, 'I would have left just before you arrived.' The look of surprise on the face of the minister next to him was a picture concluded Erwin. Erwin and Anne both chuckled at this. It was clear to me that this was an incident that Erwin had recounted on many occasions. It was again another example of how able Erwin was at playing someone along, an entertaining game for him that would catch the other person out, but it was not without some humour, nonetheless. It also gave me more confidence that Erwin would probably disclose more of his story at a time of his choosing. Any questions I had of him would have to be carefully framed and timed. It would be better to just walk beside him and allow him to decide what and when he wanted to share aspects of his story, if anything.

Chapter 5

ANOTHER EVENT, ANOTHER ENCOUNTER (2006)

My dream of hosting the *Anne Frank and You* exhibition in Taunton came into being during Lent 2006. It was part of my strategy to counter the rise of the far-right in Taunton. The BNP (British National Party) were doing better than I would have liked in local polling and I considered it my duty to win over the hearts and minds of a rising generation. Just as the Holocaust Memorial Day events were not only a commemoration of the past but a lesson for the present, so the *Anne Frank and You* exhibition was to be a project like no other for the Methodist churches in the Taunton and Bridgwater area. Nothing on this scale had been undertaken by them before.

My vision of bringing the *Anne Frank and You* exhibition to Taunton had its roots in my first encounter with an earlier Anne Frank exhibition in Manchester in 1987, the year I left theological college. I recall walking round the exhibition in the City Art Gallery in silence. There were few others present. I and my father-in-law walked through it without conversation. The exhibits seemed cluttered, hastily arranged even, and the artwork accompanying it somewhat random. Nevertheless, it felt as if I were coming face to face for the very first time with the catastrophe that was the Holocaust. The exhibition achieved its intention: it thoroughly gripped me. The link with a teenage girl in a hiding place, whom I had only briefly considered previously, became very strong. I had been moved by snippets of her diary when I first found them in an anthology some years before, but to have the images and the story so starkly before me ensured that my life had taken a turning point. In a cathedral, a few years later, I saw another Anne Frank exhibition, *Anne Frank in the World*. This exhibition was far better presented than the one I had seen in Manchester. Not only did this one grip me as before, but I left with a sense of needing to do something like it in the future. The opportunity to do so came in 2006. The aim was to attract around 2 - 3,000 visitors over a three-and-a-half-week period. Some in the congregation thought this over-ambitious, a few even scoffed at the thought. More disappointingly, one told me, even as the exhibition was being erected, that this sort of thing should not be taking place in a church. She was standing at the foot of the stairs and about to leave the building. I, a few steps up the stairs heading to my office on the first floor, asked if she could give me a good reason why challenging prejudice should not be a feature of a church in the twenty-first century. She stared at me, informed me that a friend of hers had foreign neighbours and it was 'not very pleasant'. She then turned on her heels and left. My interlocuter had given me ample evidence why such an exhibition should be held in a church after all.

Whilst her view seemed to reflect that of a growing number in the wider community it was thankfully very much a minority one within the church. Indeed, members of other churches in the area came together as never before, with almost dozens of volunteers training to be guides, bookshop assistants, school liaison officers, and members of the marketing team or management team. Holocaust survivors from around the UK visited schools across the county. The target of reaching 2-3,000 people was met in the first week. At the end of the exhibition no fewer than 10,000 people had passed through the church doors, more than half of them under 18 years of age. What we were witnessing was something extraordinary: coaches of schoolchildren would pull up outside the building every day during the week and some of those children would return at weekends bringing with them members of their family. I think it is safe to say that the event had made an impression on the young people of the town and beyond.

Part of the programme for the Anne Frank exhibition were three major fringe events. The first was with Gisela Feldman and Rabbi Brian Fox. Gisela spoke of her experience on the *St Louis* as it sailed west across the Atlantic and back again with its Jewish passengers seeking the refuge that had been promised them in the Americas. Gisela, her sister, and mother were able to find passage to England and the three of them survived. Of the 900, 250 were eventually murdered by the Nazis. As part of the same presentation, Rabbi Fox followed on from this by addressing the impact of the Holocaust on theology.

A second evening was with Micheal O'Siadhail, the Irish award-winning poet whom we had flown over from Dublin especially for the event. Micheal had recently published his extraordinary collection of his poems on the Holocaust, *The Gossamer Wall.*[iii]

It was at the third event that Erwin challenged one of the speakers. This event had its origins in a conversation I had held following another Holocaust Memorial event in 2005, a year after the one that I had first met Erwin.

Holocaust Memorial Day 2005 was commemorated not at Queens College, as it had been the previous year, but in St John the Evangelist Church, one of the parish churches in the town centre of Taunton. It was situated on the opposite side of the road to one corner of the Somerset County Council buildings. It had been felt that the students at the school should still hold their own event, but if a greater impact was to be made upon the wider community the event should be held at a more accessible venue. So it was that the priest in charge of St John's and I met to consider the way forward. He was to conduct the event, and I was to speak at it. The decision paid off. More than 200 people, from offices and shops, residents near and far, gathered in the church for the forty-five-minute act of remembrance and ended with a commitment to helping the world become a better place.

As in the previous year, I was again confronted at the end. On this occasion I had not even reached the door when I was stopped in my tracks. In fact, I was still seated in my pew. Erwin was not present that day, but Thea was. (NB Thea is not her real name. I lost contact with 'Thea' a few years later.) I did not know Thea, but she was quick to introduce herself by name with an outstretched hand ready to shake mine as soon as I got over the initial shock of being spoken to by someone with such confidence and boldness!

'I've never heard an Englishman speak like that before on such important issues. We need to talk. I am from Germany. My name is Thea. I have my own story to tell. Let's have lunch. I have written my telephone number on here. Ring me.' Thea handed me the programme from the event with her name and telephone number written on it. This was all before I could respond in any way.

I recount this in great fondness for Thea. Her enthusiasm and directness was refreshing and positive, I could not help but be inspired by her energy and desire to do something. There was an animated openness that had not been present in my encounter with Erwin a year before. There was no posturing or enquiry, it was full on, matter of fact, no hesitation, and with a confidence that everything would be okay. Over the next week or so I tried to work out Thea's age in order that I might identify something of her context. I guessed mid-30s so her grandparents' generation would have experienced the Second World War.

Thea and I met for lunch as she had instructed. She insisted on paying. She spoke without many pauses. I found her gusto still as intriguing as in our first encounter. As a teenager at school, in Dusseldorf, she had been influenced by a teacher who had encouraged his students to learn all they could about their nation's darkest episode. They had together put on a major exhibition which included testimonies of those who had lived through such times. On leaving school Thea felt driven to spend time on a kibbutz in Israel. She was keen to be of help in any way she could. She reminded me that during the Holocaust Memorial Day event I had shared my dream of bringing the *Anne Frank and You* exhibition to Taunton and influencing a rising generation. Whether I liked it or not, Thea was going to be a part of it, of that she was certain. She was sure it would be an exciting project. I was still reeling from her confidence but growing ever more stirred by her enthusiasm. Here was a young German woman whose grandparents had lived through the Third Reich wanting to do what she could to make the world aware of what happens when prejudice and hostility toward the other get out of hand. Would she be of help in administration or marketing? Possibly. Then, after a while, a risky venture entered my mind. What if she and a small number of her friends, were able to speak about growing up in Germany in the post-war period, in the shadow of the Holocaust? Thea loved the idea; the only problem would be getting others to agree.

A few weeks later, Thea invited me to her home so that I could meet a few of her friends from Germany who had become resident in the Taunton area. On that evening, I arrived five minutes before the agreed time, only to find that everyone else had already gathered. Thea introduced me to her three friends, all women, perhaps one younger, the other two older. I sensed that there was a degree of tension, concern, suspicion even. I understood that. I would have been surprised had there not have been. At first, it felt a little awkward, but I believed the cause to be too important not to explore the possibility of post-war Germans sharing their experiences. I was fully aware of the extraordinary lengths West Germany, in the first decades after the war, had addressed its recent history. Indeed, I felt that Germany had addressed the dark episodes in its history better than most nations, including my own.

Thea brought in tea, coffee, and biscuits. Having introduced myself, and Thea giving me an effusive character reference, questions were asked of me. Why was the church hosting the exhibition? What was my interest in all this? Where had my inspiration come from? Following this initial 'interview' a general conversation then got underway amongst Thea's friends, about their respective jobs or families, absolutely nothing to do with the exhibition or the suggested presentation. I stayed quiet during this conversation and for much of the remaining time. I was now an onlooker from the chair near the window, with Thea kneeling on the floor to my left, two friends on the settee beyond her and another on a chair like the one I was on directly facing me. We agreed to meet again. I counted that as a positive outcome.

On the next occasion we met I arrived to discover we no longer had the comfort of the living room chairs but gathered around Thea's kitchen table. Again, everyone who was going to be in attendance had arrived before me. One of those who had been present previously was not there, but another had taken her place. This time there was cake. This time we began to look at the issues. The focus was no longer on the reason why I was keen to host an exhibition on the Holocaust, but on their own experiences and understanding: how they regarded the war and their nation's role within it; when each first became aware of the Holocaust and their immediate reactions; even whether they had asked their parents or grandparents what they had done during those times.

For one attendee such an enquiry had initiated a breakdown in her relationship with her parents that never fully healed. For another it had created a more mature and empathetic connection with her family. It became clear that there were as many responses to becoming aware of the Holocaust as there were people around the table, and no doubt many more from others beyond it. Nonetheless, we then explored what *we* were seeking to achieve by speaking about these things in public; note that the emphasis was now on the third person plural, not *my* aims in doing so. This was of course something none of them had done before, at least not to a group of people who would be in the main British. There was still a mountain to climb before the group was ready to commit to the event, but each was willing to meet again.

It was at the third gathering that the group agreed to proceed with the presentation. However, the format, the programme, was going to be important. Even the layout of the room needed serious consideration. Despite thinking there may be forty to fifty people that would come to such an event, one of my new friends suggested we take to the venue Thea's kitchen table, around which we had gathered and even the chairs upon which we had sat for two of the meetings. Even the vase and flowers from the table would have to be taken along, so too the biscuits. It was suggested we should sit in almost the same positions around the table as we had done in Thea's kitchen – I say 'almost' because we could not have anyone's back to the audience. It was also proposed we carry on our conversation as if we were still in Thea's kitchen with the audience merely onlookers witnessing it. These proposals were met with unanimous approval, and we had a good laugh about it.

The transformation over just three gatherings was astonishing. One of our friends had previously been sceptical of the whole venture but was now able to say that she was looking forward to it; she wanted non-Germans to know what it was like to be 'burdened' with her nation's past. Another said she felt less burdened than others about her own family's Second World War story and was therefore often annoyed that the German perspective was never properly addressed. The two positions seemed to highlight the range of experience and opinion.

Part of the reason for such a spectrum of views was down to when each was born because this tended to determine the prevailing approach to the war that had existed during their formative years, especially in schools. One then told us of her first meeting with her future in-laws some years before. She had met the man who was to become her husband while he was in Germany serving in the RAF. He invited her to meet his parents in England. As they finished their first meal together the mother of her then boyfriend suggested they clear away the dishes later so that they could first go and sit in the lounge because they loved to watch a particular comedy on TV. It happened to be Fawlty Towers. The main character was Basil Fawlty, the scatty and often rude proprietor of the small fictitious hotel Fawlty Towers. What the future in-laws did not realise was that night's episode would include Basil's offensive attitudes to some German guests, broadcast for the very first time. The parents had probably intended the experience of watching a British TV comedy with their son's German girlfriend to be a bonding experience. However, it soon became thoroughly awkward for them as Basil Fawlty goose-stepped across the hotel dining room shouting 'Don't mention the war.' The girlfriend, young and fresh from Germany, found it thoroughly amusing. So too did everyone else around Thea's kitchen table as she recounted her future parents-in-law's embarrassment. Someone said it would be wonderful to begin the presentation in church with this very clip. I really was very unsure; but those around me became adamant. What could I do?

The evening of the event arrived. Four post-war German women and I seated on Thea's kitchen chairs, gathered around Thea's kitchen table, with a vase of flowers and biscuits on it, in the area usually occupied by a communion table. I introduced those alongside me and then mentioned we were to begin the evening with a video clip on the big screen. The four German women laughed openly as they watched again John Cleese satirically drawing attention to the absurdity of British prejudice towards Germans. The look on the faces of the audience that night in church, not the forty or fifty as we had initially thought, but around 120, was something to behold. For much of the audience there was great uncertainty, and for some even shock. In the comfort and secrecy of their own homes they had probably laughed at this episode or similarly stereotypical presentations of Germans and the British attitude toward them over the years since the war. This is how we began the evening, without any advance warning from me what the clip we were about to watch was about. I doubt anyone in the church that night, knowing they were to hear from post-war Germans speaking about the Holocaust and its aftermath, would have expected Basil Fawlty to appear on the screen being his exaggeratedly obnoxious, racist self. They had come to hear perspectives from Germans, not be so cogently reminded of British prejudice toward them.

That is how the night began. It would end with, what was for me a sort of *déjà vu,* almost. On this occasion however, I was a spectator and not on the receiving end of Erwin's question. I spotted Erwin rise the minute the event concluded just as he must have done two years previously, but this time he did not approach me, instead he went directly over to one of the speakers. With his wife Anne at his side, he asked the speaker what they would have done given the circumstances of the 1930s and '40s.

In the intervening hour and a half each of the four speakers had recounted what it was like to grow up in the post-war period. They recalled how they had first come to hear of the Holocaust: one from a friend at school, another from a book. Two spoke of how they had confronted their parents with their new-found knowledge. One spoke of shame and how she had addressed it. Another said how as a teacher in England she had led a school assembly on Remembrance Day and had put a slide on the screen of her father in his wartime uniform much to the great surprise of the students gathered before her. Each speaker agreed the importance of learning from history and that the mistakes of the past should not be repeated. It was an extraordinary occasion.

It was a night of openness, and I believe of growth for many of those present. Thea told me later that some members of the *Somerset Deutsch Club* had initially been very suspicious of the whole idea, concerned about Germans baring their souls before a non-German audience. However, she said, some who had been unconvinced to begin with had been won over by the occasion itself. Interestingly most of the *Club* had sat at the back. I knew that Erwin was far from sure about the whole event but attended and had again sat just a few rows from the front. What the women had to say clearly disturbed him. He later told me that 'those girls (sic) just don't understand. They have no idea what it was like. They don't know what their parents and grandparents had to go through.' I did not feel it right for me to comment, let alone judge. However, what was confirmed for me was that I still did not know Erwin sufficiently well enough to be confident of where he stood. Consequently, I became convinced that it was right not to invite him to speak on a similar occasion, not just because I was not sure where he would take his audience but also for his own sake. Even though he had told me that he had recounted his PoW experiences to several church groups over the years, I still did not feel it appropriate for him to do so as we sought to raise awareness of the Holocaust and its lessons for the twenty-first century. This was partly because he was still very bitter at how he and his comrades had been treated by the British as Prisoners of War, which to many would have sounded deeply ironic. Additionally, I admit, my decision may still have had something to do with my own discomfort at knowing someone who may have had a darker story than I had hitherto been aware of. Whether I was right or had missed an opportunity remained to be seen.

Chapter 6

A DEFINING DISCLOSURE

'We didn't know this was happening. How could we?' Erwin was still smarting over the event at which four German women, born after the war, spoke of their experiences growing up in the dark shadow of the Holocaust and their parents' and grandparents' generations' perceived complicity. Both he and Anne sat resolute in their chairs. Anne's eyes firmly fixed, lips sealed. Erwin with a demeanour that was almost imploring me to believe him. Our relationship had undoubtedly taken a turn. There was a grim determination in Erwin's body language, a resolve in his voice. I sensed he felt I was somehow responsible for a kind of betrayal. I did not detect any shame or regret on Erwin's part as we faced one another, yet just a week before the young women had displayed shame and regret in bucketsful.

Erwin and I had met numerous times over the previous two years without anything resembling the tension we now experienced in his and Anne's lounge. We had grown accustomed to my occasional presence in their home and comfortable in each other's company. The conversations had reached a point that one could describe them as almost mundane – in one sense not that different to any I would hold with most of my congregants. We would discuss the weather, ailments, family, church, and the political situation without going into too much depth. However, Erwin and Anne were not members of any of the churches I served as a minister. So, although the nature of the conversations bore some resemblance to those that I held with my elderly congregants, they always had a different feel to them.

Due to the demands on my diary as a minister, I did not have many opportunities to visit church members on a regular basis let alone those who were not attending. However, I always tried to fit Erwin and Anne into regular, if not frequent visits. It was during these visits that I became aware of the fact that Erwin and Anne had not been blessed with children. On one occasion Erwin admitted that he did have a son by a previous and temporary relationship. 'These things happen you know. We were young. We made mistakes,' he had said. I was told that the relationship between Erwin and his son was almost non-existent. He had not seen him for several years. He had occasionally but rarely made contact. Some years later Erwin informed me of his son's early death at around 60. Following Erwin's death, a close friend of his said Erwin believed his son was gay and that this had not been something Erwin could come to terms with. This would certainly fit with Erwin's comment to me that he could not accept his son's lifestyle. It was not the only occasion when Erwin's strict upbringing with his Salvationist father may have played a part in his thinking.

Meeting with Erwin just days after his attendance at the event where the four younger women had spoken of growing up in the shadow of the Holocaust was a salutary reminder that Erwin was not one of my regular church members, indeed he was no ordinary neighbour. I had never met anyone like him before, nor someone with his back story. I knew that Erwin had served in Ukraine. I felt confident in my assumption that he was in the SS in some capacity due to the account he had given me of removing his insignia on capture. The massacres in Ukraine and elsewhere in occupied territories during the Second World War were frequent and huge. How could he have not known anything? Or when he claimed he did not know was he only referring to the death camps themselves? 'We didn't know this was happening. How could we?' So, I decided that this was the opportunity to challenge him directly, it would be the first time I did so. Many other occasions would present themselves in the coming years, but I could not have known that at the time. For all I knew this could spell the end of our conversations. It was a risk I was prepared to take because I owed it to the Holocaust survivors I had met in previous years and in some cases had become friends with. Delving in, I asked him directly about the camps. I stated that I was aware of German PoWs in the UK being shown newsreel footage of Bergen-Belsen shortly after its liberation and asked if he could recall being shown such a film. The answer was unequivocal: no, he could not remember anything of the kind. I found this surprising to say the least. Surely the horrific scenes that would have been presented to the prisoners would shock them. Unless, of course, they had known about the camps all along, or had witnessed similarly horrific scenes themselves, or had just erased the footage from memory. Perhaps Erwin was being partially honest in his responses, perhaps he had not known about the cattle trucks crammed with Jews, the selections on the ramp, children torn from their parents, wives from their husbands. Perhaps he had not known about the gas chambers, the smell of roasted flesh, the piles of shoes, hair, gold teeth, spectacles, and suitcases. Perhaps he had not known about these things. Perhaps he could not recall being made to sit in a hut to watch newsreel footage from Belsen as thousands of rotting bodies were bulldozed into mass graves, as the former guards were forced to participate in the collection of bodies, or the locals being marched past the scenes of utter desecration of the human body. Perhaps it all passed him by as so many claimed. Perhaps he simply could not recall. Perhaps he had shut it out of his mind and 60 years later remained oblivious.

However, it seemed odd to me that Erwin knew absolutely nothing or could not recall anything. Some years later this was to play on my mind and lead me to think that someone who claimed to have not seen or heard of such atrocities had much to hide. Why had he made such a claim? I cannot say for sure; several factors could have been at play. However, what did he know? What had he witnessed? What could he recall? Where had he been exactly? What had he done?

Thankfully our relationship did not end there, as I had initially feared. Clearly my boldness in being so direct had not put Erwin off talking to me. Therefore, on another visit when he and Anne were less angry about the presentation by the post-war generation German women and less defensive about his wartime experiences, I went on to ask him about his time in Ukraine. What was it like? Had he lost friends there?

Getting alongside Erwin, or perhaps it is more accurate to say being allowed to get alongside Erwin, was only possible by approaching him without a sense of judgment. It was far more productive to have a 'healthy' interest in the man, in what it was that made him tick, or how he had been impacted by the war. How had he survived? How had he addressed what was obvious to any rational person that the regime he fought for had been evil to the core? To even begin to unpeel the layers that protected Erwin's perspectives on the past, one had to become party to his joy in bartering, a skill at which he was very much an expert. This was evidenced, of course, during the exchange of his watch and eventually the key for tins of corned beef and biscuits respectively in a holding camp. Even whilst accepting this approach I was confident he knew I wasn't as green as the young British guard in northern France, but that I too was playing the same cat and mouse game he wanted to engage in, which is another reason perhaps why he so enjoyed our *tête-à-têtes*: they occasionally resembled a kind of conversational chess, a game that he very much enjoyed. There was a little bit of story here, and a withholding of information there. He knew, and I slowly grew to know, when to change subject or call the engagement to a halt altogether. This was something Erwin was especially adept at, and we both knew it. In fact, over the years, especially so towards the end of his life and when I had become much more aware of his role in the SS, Erwin continued to display an extraordinary ability to change the subject when I was getting too close to a disclosure on his part. I realised early on that this was probably going to be a long game, and so it turned out to be, but longer than I could have ever imagined at that point.

Alongside my conversations with Erwin, I was still seizing every opportunity to sit with the last British veterans of the Second World War and Holocaust survivors. Even in the early years of the twenty-first century many were being taken from us and their stories remained untold. I had the sad but great privilege of conducting funerals for veterans of Dunkirk, El Alamein, D-Day, as well as Bomber Command. Sometimes with a bereaved family I shared a particular story their recently deceased relative had shared with me only to discover that the family had not been aware of it before. It often became important for them that the newly known story was recounted in the funeral address, a form of tribute to their loved one.

I was cognisant of veterans keeping their wartime experiences from their loved ones in their lifetime, yet willing to share them with me almost certainly knowing that I would probably later recount the story at their funeral. There were many reasons why they should withhold their story from their loved ones, not least their own trauma. However, they sometimes chose not to do so because they did not want to experience their family's response to hearing what they had gone through; in other words, they 'hid' their story from their family to protect them from what they had witnessed or participated in.

Veterans withholding their wartime experience from loved ones became especially apparent to me in May 1995 on the fiftieth anniversary of VE Day. The church I was serving at that time held a celebratory weekend. It was in the weeks leading up to the event and during the weekend itself that some of the wartime stories from the congregation came pouring out for the first time. Two women who had been part of the congregation for many years discovered they had both worked at Bletchley Park. Owing to the wartime secrecy of the establishment they had hardly mentioned their involvement to anyone. One man, after fifty years, finally informed his wife why it was he had nightmares so often and had to switch the TV off whenever film footage of the

Holocaust was broadcast: he had been one of the first British soldiers to enter the camp at Belsen.

All these stories played in my mind alongside the first person accounts I had heard from Auschwitz survivors, *Kindertransportees*, and even two sisters, one referred to earlier, who had been aboard the *St Louis*. I had heard stories, testimonies, horrific accounts, and I was aware that many, many more stories would never be told, they would remain buried deep in the minds of those who had experienced them and would never be recounted to anyone. The clock was ticking, in a few years there would be no one left to speak of their experience in the war. Therefore, I increasingly felt it my duty to be a person that could offer a listening ear to anyone who wanted or needed to tell something of their story.

Erwin was of course unique in my personal experience. He was the only German veteran that I had been able to sit down with and engage in conversation. Additionally, he was almost certainly a former member of the SS, though I was still a long way from proving it, let alone him admitting it. In the meantime, consequently, I was available should Erwin want to share his experiences with me.

According to Erwin, the 'girls,' as he called the four that had bared their souls so publicly, knew nothing of what his generation had faced. They did not know what it was like to watch their mother struggling to provide for her children with what little there was available; or to see their father without work or purpose. 'The girls' could never appreciate the pride that returned to Germans after Hitler had become Chancellor, the joy on the streets, the hope he gave them. 'The girls' had only known the post-war German economic miracle. However, I found it more than a little frustrating that Erwin failed to acknowledge at this stage in our conversations the destruction the Nazis had brought to Germany and the rest of Europe. Not once in my hearing was Erwin able to admit that the pride and hope he believed Hitler had brought to the German people was based on an ideology of hatred, division, and destruction. In his view, 'the girls' had expressed shame and remorse in their parents' and grandparents' generation without fully appreciating what that generation had experienced because 'the girls' themselves had not been alive to witness it.

So, what had Erwin witnessed? I put this question to him. What had he faced exactly?

'I came close to losing my life. But the Lord protected me. I always read my Bible and said my prayers. It was thanks to the Lord that I survived.'

Erwin went on to tell me that on one occasion he and three others, a gun detachment, had dug in, but took a direct hit. One of the four was killed outright, one lost an arm, the other was also badly hurt. Erwin was unscathed because, of course, 'the Lord had protected' him.

Then came a revelation that I have dwelt on ever since. On hearing it I felt a shiver down my spine. I could see that Erwin entered a dark place in his mind. His body went very still, and he spoke quietly. He looked down at the floor, which was unusual for Erwin because he preferred eye contact, and the more direct the better. I could then see that he had closed his eyes and screwed them up. Erwin spoke of his unit entering a village. Only women and children remained there, the men were no longer present. They went into a house. The women in the house ushered them to the table and presented them with bread and hot drinks. Erwin's voice went quieter still as he recalled sitting there, eating and drinking, looking at the women, and wondering why they were doing this when they would surely have known the soldiers had come to kill them and their families.

I could not follow this up. I sat in stony silence. I felt I was six feet away from a wartime massacre in Ukraine. The darkness of a peasant hut filled the room. The pleading faces were before my eyes. The screams pierced my ears. Many years later amongst the cache of photographic negatives Erwin gave to me there was one of two women sitting in a kitchen. When I showed the developed image to Erwin, he thought it had been taken in Ukraine. I am confident it was not from the day Erwin had recalled the futility of women offering hospitality to their likely killers, because this photograph caught relaxed, smiling faces. Nevertheless, it indicates the intimacy and trust shown by some Ukrainians to the occupying forces (Plate 4).

As Erwin recounted this incident with me, Anne had been in the kitchen completely unaware of what he had just told me. A part of me wanted to believe that Erwin's thoughts that day in Ukraine had not been as specific as I feared, in other words that Erwin and his comrades had not come to kill this family but those countrymen whom they were fighting. Then my mind would again consider the possibility that the hospitality was a plea by the family to leave them unharmed and for Erwin and his comrades to move on. However, if Erwin's mood was anything to go by, as he recounted that day from more than six decades before, I feared the worst. When I returned to this conversation later and reminded Erwin of the hospitality shown by the women, he hastily changed the subject.

When Erwin first shared this memory, hinting at the murder of civilians, I was especially shaken because of my experience in Kosovo just a few years previously. Between 1999 and 2002 when I still resided in Manchester, I helped coordinate the work of a refugee centre for more than sixty Kosovan Albanian refugees. Some of those at the centre had survived a massacre in Podujeva. In 2001, I had visited Kosovo and stood at what had been the mass grave containing the bodies of their family members. An atrocity was not a matter of history for me, nor a distant memory of a Holocaust survivor, but a recent experience for those I was closely linked with emotionally. Hearing Erwin speak as he did brought back for me the building from which a family had been led, the wall still scarred with bullet holes, the silence of the field, and the deep indescribable pain of those who stood with me that day in Podujeva just a few years earlier.

No, according to Erwin, 'the girls' who had spoken to a mainly non-German audience some weeks before could not understand Erwin's generation, not fully. No. From my perspective nor could Erwin understand theirs. They were of two different mind-sets born and raised on the same plot of land, decades apart, but whose cities, culture, and education were alien to each other. Such was the gulf between them that it seemed impossible to bridge. Too much had happened between Erwin's youth and their own. The sham of Nuremberg rallies, the uniforms that built pride in the wearer but sent fear through the spines of their victims were from a different era. The evil regime, the industrialised killing in terms of both magnitude and method, cast a shadow over succeeding generations of Germans. The utter destruction of a once proud nation with its symphony halls, museums, art galleries, universities, and commerce had left its indelible mark on those who were born there in the first few decades after defeat. Those twelve years of Nazi rule, 1933-45, had become a defining point in German history. Everything leading up to those years would become interpreted in the light, or perhaps darkness, of what was to come; and everything thereafter would be tainted by that period.

The clip of Basil Fawlty, played by John Cleese, goose-stepping across the dining room of Fawlty Towers, forefinger horizontal under his nose replicating a Hitler moustache, and screaming 'don't mention the war' at the German guests had triggered something deep within Erwin, understandably so. The four women had sought to raise awareness among the non-Germans in the audience, in a humorous way, of the ongoing presence of prejudice amongst the British towards Germans, just as John Cleese had intended. This, together with recounting their own experiences of challenging their parents, had in fact touched a raw nerve of the one German in the audience for whom the war could never be forgotten, and any mention of it took him back to those defining years of his own life.

Recounting the incident in the Ukrainian village would be the last time for many years that Erwin would permit me to enter the dark memories he had harboured for decades. For the next five years I continued to visit him and Anne, but less frequently. Our relationship always seemed warm whenever we chatted on the phone or on the increasingly rare visit, but it did not have the same momentum as it had in the earlier years. I wondered if Anne and he had discussed his attendance at the evening with the four German women. Had she shared Erwin's anger about the event? Did she warn him to be more careful about what he said to me or to others? I knew that Erwin had spoken to groups within churches and the community about his PoW years, but the experiences prior to capture had clearly remained hidden and elusive. Only once in the years we had chatted between 2004 and 2011 did he explicitly mention any form of action, the incident where his comrades were killed or maimed. Only once did he mention, with apparent regret, watching women doing what they may have thought would save them from the bullets of the soldiers before them.

When I was about to leave the West Country for a new role in Lincolnshire during the summer of 2011 and bade Erwin and Anne farewell at their doorstep, I thought that was the end of our relationship. It had been fascinating. In all honesty, despite the unusual nature of Erwin's past, I only felt connected to them in the same sense that I felt connected to many others during my ministry. I was sorry that we had not been able to share more of ourselves. Not once had Erwin asked what my grandparents had done in the war. Not once had he enquired about their stories, whether any had served, been injured, killed, or bereaved. Not once did he show the slightest interest in the possibility that my grandfathers may well have faced him in Normandy as had the unsuspecting guest preacher at the Harvest lunch in Hove all those years before. As it happened, only one of my grandfathers was conscripted into the military; he served in the Royal Marines and had to be invalided out in the summer of 1944 due to a nervous breakdown. He may well have been on the Arctic convoys to Murmansk helping to resource the very forces that engaged in battle with the Nazis along the Eastern Front.

However, none of this appeared to be of interest to Erwin – or was it avoidance? Was Erwin too ashamed to consider the possibility that he, or a comrade, may have pulled the trigger that ended a relative's life or scarred him forever in the fields of northern France? I had met numerous Normandy veterans over the course of my life. Some had fought against the Germans at Caen, where Erwin fought, as I was to discover later. My primary school teacher, Mr Pilsbury, had survived being shot in the throat by a sniper in Normandy. None of this was of interest to Erwin. Maybe I should have tackled him on it at the time, but for now the conversations appeared to be at a close. As an aside, I can recall Mr Pilsbury, Tom, because he became a lifelong friend, in the classroom in 1970 or '71, spotting through the window a magpie walking across the playground: 'Look at him,' he said. 'Magpies are the SS of the bird world – strutting their stuff in a fancy uniform, arrogant and ruthless.' What Tom would have made of Erwin and my relationship with him is anyone's guess.

Little did I know that within a year Erwin would take me by complete surprise. I had promised him and Anne that I would pop in to see them when I made my first trip back to the West Country, and I duly did. I telephoned in advance. I was to be at a conference in Plymouth for a week and on the way home I could visit them. They were delighted to see me, and in all truth I them.

Over tea and delicious homemade Welsh cakes, freshly made that day and proudly brought in by a smiling Anne, we chatted like old friends. Somehow the distance and separation had relaxed Erwin and Anne, even though a year was not so long when our visits prior to my relocation had been so sporadic. Erwin had news for me. He had been typing up his memoirs. Despite my best attempts at trying to remain a little nonchalant, as if writing a memoir was the most natural thing to do for someone who may well have served in the SS on the Eastern Front, Erwin could not possibly have missed the look of surprise and thrill that must have formed across my face at the possibility of reading his memoirs. Erwin asked if I could look at the document and edit it. He would surely have known what my response would be, but he seemed delighted to hear of my consent. However, a concern grew within me. I could not help it. What if I became aware of something that was altogether sinister? What would I do? Was I, an ordained minister, bound to confidentiality? 'It's what I speak about when I talk to groups,' Erwin explained. So, it was to be about his PoW days then? Yes. 'Oh yes,' said Erwin, 'people need to know what happened to us.'

We were almost back to my first visit to his home eight years previously in 2004. Erwin wanted to record his anger at what he perceived to be mistreatment at the hands of his British captors; which to me seemed so ironic, as I mentioned before. Then just as my emotional rollercoaster was easing off, it sped up again: 'This is volume three,' he said. Volume three? 'Yes. Volume one is my life in

Berlin in the 1930s and volume two is my time in the war – but I'm still writing those. Volume three is finished. I want you to let me know what you think. I want to get it published.'

I had very mixed feelings about being drawn into the possibility of editing Erwin's memoirs, especially if they were to gloss over the atrocities and, or, be a bitter account of his days as a PoW. Editing the memoirs of a possible member of the SS of his time in captivity was not exactly what I had in mind especially after I had listened to Holocaust survivors give accounts of their experiences, their suffering, and trauma. He was not a camp guard, of that I felt sure, nevertheless none of this was sitting easily with me.

A few months earlier I had been part of a ten-day clergy seminar at Yad Vashem, the world Holocaust Remembrance Centre in Jerusalem. We had explored many aspects of the Holocaust, from the anti-Jewish teachings of the early church, through to the growing nationalism of the nineteenth century and the Final Solution itself. While there I took the opportunity to meet with a historian who had studied the SS. When I shared with her something of my experience and knowledge of Erwin, without mentioning a name, she concluded that he was almost certainly a member of the Waffen SS. It was seven years later that I was to discover exactly which unit in the Waffen SS Erwin had belonged. Despite my misgivings, I was for now willing to do as I had been asked: read, perhaps edit, and feedback on Erwin's memoirs, volume three, 'Captivity.'

Another farewell on the doorstep. Another metaphorical carrot dangled before me with Erwin seemingly carrying on his game of cat and mouse, the game he had so expertly played with the British guard in northern France in 1944. In this instance Volume 3 was the watch, the key would have to come later. I would receive the volume in the post. I would then be in touch. We would chat on the phone. We would see each other again when I next visited the West Country.

PART II
DISCLOSURES

Chapter 7

MEMOIRS, VOLUME 3 (2012)

The incident that gave Erwin as much joy as bartering with his British guard in northern France was sabotaging the bonfire scheduled to be lit on the first anniversary of VE Day. He relayed the story to me on more than one occasion and each time it raised a chuckle in him. I could understand some of his glee, it must have brought him and his defeated comrades a sense of vengeance or *schadenfreude* when they saw the glow from the fire. Nevertheless, I could not help but feel sorry for those who had worked so hard in gathering the wood and carrying it to the beach, which had almost certainly been a community effort. No doubt, the whole city, though the smallest in the UK, would have been looking forward to celebrating the victory of a year before.

By 1946 the loss of so many, the horrors of war, and the challenge of re-constructing buildings, lives, relationships, and society had all begun to sink in. The planned commemorative occasion would have been tinged with a degree of melancholy, with deep emotions felt by those around the bonfire. But Erwin had other ideas.

He managed to persuade a pal to join him on an excursion that was to take place on the night before VE Day. The new moon was 1 May that year so when Erwin and his comrade set off from the camp six nights later it was dark, the moon having not quite reached its first quarter. Thus far it had been a cool month with temperatures below the seasonal average in that part of West Wales. There was a ground frost each morning almost throughout the month. Even allowing for the micro-climate of St David's, right on the tip of the southwest Pembrokeshire peninsula, it would have been chilly to say the least.

Erwin was in a sweater and donned cap, items which he wore as the camp goalkeeper. As I had come to know Erwin well, I could just imagine his face as he set off, with a wry smile on his lips. He had just turned twenty-six a month earlier so he would probably have still been like a teenager bent on mischief. That sense of adventure had, of course, been well honed over the course of his military service, in far more serious circumstances. Erwin's recently received memoirs (Volume 3 of course!) retold the event in detail. I have preserved the wording as he recorded it. It serves to highlight Erwin's playful nature. In later years, however, I would come to think of his light-hearted manner as a worrying indication of his almost dismissive attitude towards more serious incidents.

> In a camp in Wales, we were taken out to work for the first time. It was not a camp with barracks as we had previously, but a large country house, perhaps a mansion describes it more accurately. There were 50 of us accommodated in several bedrooms. The place was St. Davids at the extreme west point of South Wales. From there we were taken to a large nursery which had fields on both sides of a road. We were given long hoes to clear a large field of onions of weeds. Occasionally a large lorry would pass by, carrying British sailors who were ferrying large amounts of burnable rubbish to a beach nearby. Each time the lorry passed, the sailors would give the two finger sign, which we thought to be a friendly greeting. When our driver explained the real meaning, we realized it was not meant to be a friendly greeting. He also told us that the rubbish was for a bonfire to celebrate V.E. day. After questioning the driver more closely, we got to know the exact date of the celebrations. Now you would never guess what wicked thought came into my head.
>
> In the hostel we had a mixture of soldiers and sailors, and I had befriended an ex-U-boat sailor, whom I knew I could trust. When I told him about my plan to set fire to the bonfire one day prematurely, he agreed to come with me. He still had his navy uniform blazer, which would recognize him as a sailor. I had a pullover without POW markings and a flat cap, which I wore as goalkeeper of our football team.
>
> So far so good, now we had to work out the details of our plan. The hostel was quite near the beach, and we spent many hours beach-combing to find anything useful that the tide washed up. One such lot that we found earlier was a box with what appeared to be blocks of soap, but it was more of a waxy substance which, when a type of wick was inserted, could be used as a candle. That was just what we needed to light the bonfire.
>
> Perhaps I should explain something about the layout of the hostel. As I mentioned before, it was a large country mansion and there was no fencing or barbed wire around it, and we could come and go as we pleased. Well, you might say, what about escaping? Escaping where to? Remember we are on an island, and islands are generally surrounded by water – lots of water! Here is what you need if you are going to escape: you need inconspicuous-looking civilian clothing, you need outside

help if you can, you need money, you need to speak the language and a plan or map to know where you are going. You want to eat, sleep, and do other things except to be conspicuous to succeed. So as far as I was concerned, forget it.

Now back to our wicked plan. It would have been foolish to confide our intention to anybody else in the hostel, we were on our own. The night came and everything was ready. It was arranged that we would go to bed as normal (fully dressed), and get up later to leave by 11 o'clock. I was dressed like a farm worker, pair of Wellingtons, scruffy pullover and cap, my friend wore his blazer and looked every bit a sailor.

We walked along the coastal path and had about four miles to reach the bonfire site. The last 200 yards had to be on the road, and we were hoping that we would not meet anybody. The excitement mounted as we reached the big heap, and it was BIG, like a large bungalow. The preparation went well, we found a large wooden barrel, which we stuffed with wood shavings, and a few of our special candle type blocks and set them alight. The open top was covered with a piece of cardboard, and off we went. We had covered about 100 yards, when I turned to look back and saw a beam of light shining from the bung-hole, I quickly ran back and stuffed something into the hole of the barrel.

We hurried back to the hostel and arrived just before two o'clock and found everyone asleep. Very quietly we undressed not to give the show away. From our window we could see the fire burning. I pretended to come back from the toilet, made some noise to wake some of the others, to draw their attention to the large fire. This was for no other reason than to establish an alibi.

Erwin took great pride in getting away with his act of sabotage. In a sort of extension to what seemed to be a story line straight out of a Dad's Army episode, Erwin told me that no one ever discovered who had been the culprits. During another conversation some years later he was to claim, with as much of a chuckle as he had had when he first described the story for me, who the local community blamed for the premature bonfire. The local bus driver or conductor, who had been in the pub that night had apparently drunk one or two too many and let their emotions get ahead of themselves.[iv]

On reading Volume 3 of Erwin's memoirs for the first time I was able to add more details to the accounts he had shared with me previously. Erwin said he had sent a copy to me because initially he wanted me to edit it and advise him should he again be asked to speak to a group on his days as a PoW. Despite my earlier reticence I became willing to fulfil his request because I felt it important for a record to be kept of his experiences. However, his memories were probably little different to the tens of thousands of German PoWs that had been brought to the UK. These men were kept long after the war to work on farms, with some choosing to settle here having met women who would eventually become their wives. Nevertheless, I felt a sense of duty, even some kind of loyalty, to Erwin. It had been Erwin who had initiated the conversation at the Holocaust Memorial Day event in 2004, and he had been a willing partner in nurturing our friendship over the years. He always seemed to ensure there was a good reason for me to make a return visit to his home, this he did by dangling another metaphorical carrot before me as another conversation drew to a close. Those visits would become fewer over the following years, with greater gaps in between. I was now living 230 miles from Erwin, and my professional responsibilities lay in Lincolnshire, not Somerset.

Not surprisingly there were one or two minor inconsistencies in the written account of his capture and captivity compared with his oral testimony, not least whether Erwin had removed his insignia on capture or in the cell during his first night in the Brussels jail. What was consistent was the fact that he had pushed his pay book (*soldbuch*) into the palliasse (straw mattress) which, unknown to Erwin for many years, would later be retrieved and placed in the German State archives (*Bundesarchiv*). I am confident that I had remembered his first re-telling of his capture and how he had removed the insignia from his right-side lapel as soon as his fate was sealed. Did he suspect that as a member of his unit he would not be treated well by those who now had him in their grasp? Whatever the inconsistencies, minor though they were, the written account confirms Erwin's extraordinary resourcefulness.

> 'You have been captured.' To explain the meaning of these few words, I will attempt to describe to you my experience. The day was 3rd September 1944; the place was Brussels in Belgium. It was late in the afternoon when it happened. I have little recollection how and where I spent the first night. Surprised, confused, distressed, upset and humiliated are some of the emotions going through my head. Upset by the loss of life I had just witnessed, distressed at the uncertain future which is to follow. The second night was spent in a large jail in Brussels. Five of us were led to a cell that had straw-filled palliasses on the floor. Before preparing to settle down to go to sleep, I remembered the instruction received during military training, when captured you only give your name, rank and serial number. That prompted me to remove all external identifications from my uniform, and together with my pay-book, which contained all sorts of important information, stuffed the lot deep into the palliasse.

That important information of course would have indicated to his captors that he was a member of the Waffen SS. Some years later, after I had confronted Erwin with this fact and he had admitted his unit, he would fill in more details of that second night of captivity. He informed me that just after he had removed his insignia a British soldier entered the cell shouting 'SS? SS?' The soldier was waving a loaded pistol. Erwin said he may well have been drinking earlier that evening as he appeared to be drunk. The guard was certainly angry and may well have been looking for revenge. Erwin's comrades were silent. The soldier ordered Erwin to stand, and he pointed the gun at his face asking 'SS?' Erwin replied in the negative and after a few very tense moments the British soldier left the room. Erwin never saw him again. It was a lucky escape. I was later to discover that Erwin had fought at the bloody battle of Caen where little quarter was given by the Canadians towards members of the SS. Erwin would also have known how captured members of the SS were treated by the Soviets on the Eastern Front, little different, I hasten to add, to how the SS treated those they took prisoner at Caen and on the Eastern Front.

This incident in the Brussels cell was not recorded in Erwin's memoirs Volume 3 of course, as we were still some way off Erwin acknowledging he had been a member of the Waffen SS. Despite all the signals he was sending out I was still not completely sure he knew I was working things out for myself. Maybe he was, maybe he wasn't, I really could not tell. Maybe this was all part of his game. Perhaps he was waiting for me to pop the question, I will never know.

Being confronted with a pistol-wielding and intoxicated guard was the second time in as many days Erwin had come close to death, but again the earlier incident would only be disclosed to me much later.

Before the disclosure that he was a member of the SS and his sharing with me details of these two incidents, I would discover just how close Erwin came to death in combat and how he had been shunted across Nazi-occupied Europe with his unit. For now, Volume 3 was all that I had to go on. However, it provided a fascinating insight into Erwin's capacity to adapt, and it also gave numerous examples of the resourcefulness that he had developed. Exchanging a pocket watch for tins of corned beef and holding back the key for a further transaction was just one incident of many. Slightly later in captivity he ensured he was chosen for work details so that he could seek out old newspapers, almost certainly for his personal hygiene, locate a tin can for drinking and even a box to sit on. On arrival in the UK, he was wise enough to engage in some forward thinking before taking a shower by working out where to hide his wallet for retrieval later. He also pocketed empty spectacle cases that he came across for transactions. He withheld labour until the farmer treated him and his comrades better. At another farm he was receiving a cooked breakfast each morning and decided it unwise to tell other PoWs in the camp to ensure they did not get in on the act and replace him. Each of these examples tell us much about Erwin and his survival instincts.

As expected, another feature of Volume 3 detailed Erwin's sense of being treated unfairly. The conditions of the holding camps, the constant moving from one PoW camp to another,[v] consequently being unable to make friends as he claimed to be an introvert, the lack of proper pay for the work he undertook, the length of time he was held after the war, these and even more were all sources of discontent for Erwin. His list of grievances was almost endless. It was this that tested my patience more than anything and I later told him so. What did he expect? Britain and her allies had made great sacrifices to rid Europe of the evils of fascism. The country was itself impoverished, still experiencing rationing, and though victorious in war, peacetime was far from easy.

In the accounts Erwin had shared with me thus far there appeared to be little or even no remorse. Perhaps the only occasion he came anywhere near regret was the confusion he felt when women in their home near the Eastern Front showed hospitality to him and his comrades. I asked myself if, as a PoW just a few years later, his mind ever wandered back to that particular incident while eating a cooked breakfast at the kitchen table of a Welsh farmhouse waited on by Margaret, the fifteen or sixteen-year-old farmer's daughter?

> One day I was sent out to a farm by myself. Again a group of us was picked up by the driver, who distributed us to different farms. Because we were expected to work a full eight-hour-day, before leaving the camp we were each given a sandwich, consisting of two slices of half inch thick bread, filled with some meat or fish paste.
>
> I was dropped by the roadside, pointed to the farm, took my sandwich and walked to the farmhouse. Now I must emphasise, that my knowledge of the English language was not anywhere near what it is today, but I got by. When a lady opened the door after my knock I told her that I came to do some work. She asked me in and said, 'Did you not see my husband, he took the tractor up the road to pick up some machinery?' to which I answered, this is my first time here, and I don't know what your husband looks like. She realized the mistake and said you will have to wait until he comes back, come and sit down. 'Have you had breakfast?' she asked. After my hesitant answer she said, 'Margaret will make you some breakfast. It was her daughter and I guessed she was about 15 - 16 years old, but boy did she cook me a nice breakfast.

> When you get that sort of treatment, you forget completely that you are a POW.

Or, as a PoW, did he feel the cold of a Russian winter in his bones again when clearing roads of snow during the bitter winter of 1947?

> 1947 - There was heavy snow that winter and we were taken out to clear the roads. That was something I did not enjoy, fortunately, it did not last very long.

There was little self-reflection in his account of his days as a PoW. He saw no irony when describing the taking of a shower on his arrival in the UK. It was at Kempton Park racecourse no less that the newly arrived PoWs were processed.

> After a while, we could see that the processed boys were forming a unit away from us and were separately guarded. When I noticed that they were using the same toilet area, I made it my business to meet one there. That is when I learned, that after registration they had to strip naked and leave everything behind before going into the jockey's shower room to have a good wash and shave, and on the other side received fresh clothing and a special POW uniform, which was a specially adapted British military outfit, which made them easy to identify as POW's.
>
> This business of leaving everything behind made me think. How can I keep my wallet with its contents and a few other things that I did not want to lose? Put all those things under a slop-bucket when no one is present to see what you are doing, and retrieve them when you are through. It was a chance I was prepared to take in the hope that it would work.
>
> To describe the experience when I stepped into the shower is beyond all words. To receive clean underwear and a new uniform made me feel human again. I hurried to join the crowd outside and was most anxious to visit the comfort area and hopefully retrieve my things. I know that I had to be very careful not to be seen lifting the bucket, and when the coast was clear I quickly retrieved my things and thanked God for a job well done.

I found this to be extraordinary. Maybe at the time of Kempton Park, he would not have known the process of leaving personal items for collection later, stripping naked, and taking a 'shower' at Auschwitz and other camps, but he would have known this by the time he came to write his memoirs and as he described his experience to me. I admit that I found the parallel experience excruciating. Maybe I was asking too much of him? Maybe not. 'I quickly retrieved my things and thanked God for a job well done.' If only millions of Jews and countless numbers of others could have uttered the same prayer.

Having edited the document and made a few suggestions, I returned it to Erwin who telephoned me to say how delighted he was with it and how appreciative he was for what I had done. He again assured me that if anyone was to read the earlier volumes then it would be me, 'later'. Again, it was as if he needed to pique my interest, to keep me in touch with him, to guarantee that he would have at least me to hear his story, 'later' one day. However, years would pass without much else to add to the story. I would telephone him occasionally and chat warmly with Anne before she would hand me over to Erwin. We would talk about all sorts of general matters, especially health and the impact of ageing on him and Anne.

When he joined Facebook, he rang to ask if I was a member, and if we could be friends on Facebook. That gave me his birthday of course and a year did not pass without me making a quick call to wish him well and enquire after his and Anne's health and wellbeing.

At some point his only child, a son, born before he knew Anne, had died in his 60s. They had been estranged and had made only occasional contact. According to Erwin he was now left only with his niece in Germany and Anne at his side.

Chapter 8

THE TRUTH BEGINS TO UNFOLD (2019)

It was not until late 2019 that my relationship with Erwin took a new twist. It had almost faded away some time before. I had not spoken to him, even by telephone, for quite a while and I had not visited him for perhaps two years or more. In November of that year, I was sitting in a meeting with little to fully occupy my thinking; the discussion had no bearing on my situation, and my mind began to wander. Why I chose to put Erwin's name into a search engine on my laptop at that point I cannot say, I just did it without much prior thought. It had never occurred to me to do it in earlier years probably because the internet was not what it had become. In more recent years our relationship was becoming a thing of the past or at the very least on hold, so why it crossed my mind to type out his name on that particular day baffles me. It was nothing other than a spur of the moment gesture with absolutely no regard for what I might find.

After I had edited Volume 3 of his memoirs, Erwin had not been forthcoming with Volume 1 – his account of life before the war – and I doubted I would ever see Volume 2 – his war years. Since I first met Erwin fifteen years previously access to documentation through the internet had grown. In the early days it would have been pointless searching for Erwin on the web, as I noted above, so much so it would never have occurred to me to undertake such an exercise. However, by 2019 searching for information on the internet had become almost second nature and having never considered it before, I typed his name into the search engine: 'Erwin Stahlberg'.

The first result took me to a Luftwaffe ace, clearly not the Erwin I knew. So, I searched again, this time putting 'SS' next to his name. The response was almost instantaneous: 'SS-PGR.2 Stahlberg B.3.4.22

Strm.Stab d.o.b. 3.4.22'. The shock ran through me. I froze. My eyes fixed on the screen. Yes, I always suspected he was a member of the SS, his reference to the removal of his insignia told me as much fifteen years previously in 2004; but this apparent confirmation stunned me. I then wanted to double check that I had not identified another Erwin Stahlberg. I thought I was correct in thinking that his birthday was 3 April 1922, but I needed to be sure. Going on to his Facebook site I was able to quickly confirm that this was indeed his date of birth.

Within two minutes I had gone from what I thought of as a well-founded suspicion that had been in my mind for so long, to incontrovertible proof. A few more searches on the internet suggested that he was in fact a member of the LSSAH, which at that point meant absolutely nothing to me. The meeting I was attending was in danger of taking second place in my mind, so I had to resist further searches until the coffee break when I would take to the privacy of my room.

As I rose from my desk, laptop in hand, my colleague wanted to chat about something, but my mind was elsewhere. This new-found confirmation of what I had suspected for so long was disorientating me. Once safely in the privacy of my room, I resumed my search, and I was to discover that the LSSAH was in fact the Leibstandarte SS Adolf Hitler, Hitler's personal bodyguard before the war. Its leaders were responsible for the 1934 massacre of the rival Brownshirts known as the *Night of the Long Knives*. The Leibstandarte went on to commit atrocities across the southern sector of the Eastern Front, France, Italy, and Belgium. One of these was the summary execution of captured Americans in the Ardennes during the Battle of the Bulge, the infamous and well-documented Malmedy massacre. My stomach turned cold, my mind was in a whirl. Suspicion is one thing, knowledge another thing altogether. I hastily checked the date of Malmedy and was relieved that I had been correct in thinking that it had taken place after Erwin had been captured in Brussels, a full three months later on 17 December 1944. However, I could no longer ignore the fact that Erwin had indeed been in a unit that had taken part in horrendous activities. Sure, he wasn't in the Waffen SS until the summer of '41 according to my understanding, and he had been captured before the Battle of the Bulge, therefore he could not have been involved in either the massacre of British and French PoWs in a barn near Wormhoudt and Esquelbecq in northern France on 28 May 1940 prior to Dunkirk, or, as we have noted above, the Malmedy massacre. Nevertheless, in between those atrocities there were others over on the Eastern Front, where Erwin had said he had served, though where exactly I could not, at that stage, say.

The episode of entering a Ukrainian home and being served bread and drinks by women whom Erwin or his colleagues had perhaps come to kill was now all too real for me. This was no longer a story in the mind of an elderly man, his unit now had a name, a notorious one at that, and Erwin's movements during his time within it could more easily be traced through further researching that unit.

Once I became aware of this newly discovered information, for some inexplicable reason I tried to downplay it in my mind, telling myself that it was only a few references on the internet, that I could not be one hundred per cent sure, that was how I sought to come to terms with it. Yes, he had recalled, in a very dark moment, the hospitality of those who may have been about to be killed. Yes, he had ripped his insignia off his tunic, secreted his pay book in his mattress lest his unit become known to his captors. Yes, he had shown a very cagey attitude to his war service, preferring instead conversations about his PoW days. Yes, yes, yes, but I could not escape the fact that nothing other than a quick internet search had confirmed Erwin was with the 2nd Panzer Grenadier Regiment of an SS Division.

I became torn between, on the one hand doing further research, with a desire, perversely maybe, to know more, but that felt disloyal and shameful somehow, cheating even in his game of cat and mouse, and on the other hand, simply resolving to leave well alone. My thinking was supercharged with the issues that now came to the forefront of my mind. What was I to do? Follow this information up? Or lay it all to one side? I wrestled with whether I should have been more challenging toward Erwin during our past conversations. I wondered if I should have been more upfront about my suspicions at an earlier stage. I even considered the possibility that by recalling the removal of his insignia Erwin may have been wanting me to pursue it and I had failed to seize the moment. Nevertheless, I still thought Erwin might have found my enquiry impertinent at such an early stage of our acquaintance and consequently could have shut the conversations down.

I had chosen to undertake the long path, and maybe, just maybe, I wasn't as eager to know his full story as I occasionally thought I was. Perhaps knowing the truth of Erwin's service at an early stage in our conversations would have brought me to a dark place in my mind and maybe even filled me with shame at what I was discovering and doing.

In the light of this new knowledge, this confirmation of my early suspicions, I began to wonder what lay ahead for us. How could I face him again without addressing what I had uncovered? Yet, it was surely his secret alone to share with me, should he have wished to do so, not for me to suddenly, after so long a silence, confront him with it. Yet, how could I not inform him? On the one hand, why shouldn't I be upfront with him? On the other, what good would that do? I had not seen him and Anne for a few years. Surely, it would have been inappropriate for me to just turn up on their doorstep after so long. How frail were they? Would challenging Erwin be responsible for a serious deterioration in their wellbeing? Even if I were to ring him up to rekindle our acquaintanceship, would I be acting dishonourably in that I now had an ulterior motive? Would I simply be engaging in a selfish 'I was right all along' scenario? A form of self-justification? That the man I had chatted with over so many years was no ordinary German veteran and no ordinary neighbour after all.

So many questions; so many issues; so many moral dilemmas. I concluded that I should leave well alone. That was it. We had not spoken for so long and we had not seen each other for several years. Why should I go wading in now? What good would be achieved?

I was resolved to lay it all aside; to put it all behind me. There would be no more phone calls on 3 April to pass on birthday greetings to Erwin. By my own reckoning Erwin must have been 97 at that stage, Anne younger but they would both surely be frail by now. I was not confident either would be up for a conversation, that is how I was justifying my planned withdrawal. In any case I convinced myself that he had probably told me all he wanted me to know, and he did not want to disclose anything more. I was not going to press him, if that was his story, that was his story. Further details would remain in the past; he would no doubt take them with him to the grave. This I believed, to be especially so should Anne outlive him. Even if volumes one and two of Erwin's memoirs had been written, I could not be sure Anne would not destroy them before anyone could read them. Additionally, I often considered the possibility that Erwin might not be able to keep his own promise of passing his memoirs on to me.

So, I decided to get on with my life, just as I had in previous years, without thinking much more of Erwin. I tried to put to the back of my mind that Erwin had been a member of one of the most feared units of Nazi aggression. I did not need to know any more, I knew enough, and my focus would remain with the victims and not the oppressors.

Then the phone call came, without warning, taking me by complete surprise.

Chapter 9

THE CONVERSATION RESUMES (2020)

As we know, the Coronavirus pandemic that began in 2020 changed much. There was a collective awakening, a growing awareness of the vulnerability of society, and even of individual mortality. On the morning of 13 March, ten days before the lockdown in the UK was announced, just as events were being postponed or cancelled, my telephone rang. The call was to revive my acquaintanceship with Erwin and re-ignite my interest in his story.

'Do you know who this is?' It had been a few years since we had last spoken as I had only been wishing him well for his birthday via a Facebook message. However, the voice was unmistakable, the accent as distinct as ever. It may have betrayed his age a little more than that first encounter more than sixteen years previously after the Holocaust Memorial Day event. However, it was not just the accent, it was the character holding the phone, a little mischief in the question. I could picture the glint in his eye and the apparent kindly, yet knowing, smirk on his lips. It did not take much for me to conjure up the man in my mind, or the room in which he was sitting.

'I wanted you to know that I have always seen you as a friend.' This was candid for Erwin. He had displayed a degree of friendship and trust before, but this was different, it was straight in yes, as he had been on occasions, but this was a rare admission in a certain tone of voice that hinted at genuine affection. It did not seem to be more evidence of the game he so often played, drawing me in to elicit interest. The sentence and the voice expressing it sounded open, warm, and sincerely conveyed, of that there seemed little doubt. This was a man about to become 98, I sensed he was making a statement he felt he needed to make. As a minister I had heard such declarations and sentiment before, it was part of the reckoning, it was about legacy, it was ensuring all was said and done that could be said and done while there was still time. I believe this could be detected within the voice on the other end of the phone line that evening.

Erwin informed me that Anne had died the previous October. Later I was to reflect on the possibility that the funeral must have taken place around the time I was doing an internet search for Erwin's name and making my discovery. Coincidence perhaps, but it still sent a chill down my spine, and maybe providence was at work. Erwin was still in the bungalow he and Anne had made their home. He informed me that he had daily ongoing care from visiting nurses. Generally speaking, he was in good health, but he would not live through the pandemic, of that he was certain. He said he wanted to make contact again after so long.

Now that Anne had died, I knew Erwin would no longer have any relative in the UK so I became concerned should anything happen to him, especially as I feared the forthcoming pandemic would take many lives. I enquired about his niece in Germany. He asked if he could send her my email address so that she could make contact when 'the time came'. For Erwin it was important that I be kept informed.

Later that same day, at lunchtime, I dropped Erwin an email to say how good it was to hear his voice, to express sadness at Anne's death, and to confirm that I was happy for him to pass on my email address, indeed, I suggested it might be good if I were to have hers too.

Within ten minutes, Erwin had replied with the email address of his niece. I wrote to her a few days later having got my letter translated, as Erwin informed me that she didn't speak much English. The email bounced back. Maybe the email address Erwin had given me contained an error. I mentioned this to him on the phone a day later. Erwin simply responded with one of his chuckles. Had Erwin, I wondered, deliberately put up obstacles before me in order that I did not converse with someone whom I was to discover had known something of his story and his membership of the SS many years previously? Again, I will never know, but with hindsight it certainly feels that way. Potentially an inaccurate email address and the claim that his niece did not speak much English seemed pure Erwin in playful mood, protecting his identity for as long as possible.

As the Covid lockdown commenced, I spent much time telephoning the vulnerable and those at risk seeking to ensure they had food and other provisions. Isolation was affecting people's wellbeing. Understandably, there was fear in the voices of many. It became natural to add to my list of people to contact a small number of people from my past, Erwin included.

The conversations with others tended to be around what was in place for their food supply, the collection of prescriptions, what they would do if they fell ill, and the wellbeing of their families, who were often at a distance. With Erwin, the conversations over those first weeks of the Covid lockdown were different. There was an urgency about them. There was a tying up of loose ends. There was the conviction on the part of Erwin that he would not live through the pandemic. Therefore, at the end of April 2020 it seemed natural for me to ask whether Erwin had ever written down his memoirs from before his capture as he said he would some years before. Yes, he had. Yes, they were on his computer. Did he want those memoirs to be read at some point? Yes, after, after he had 'closed (his) eyes for the last time' – this was a phrase he would come to use several times over his final years. Were the memoirs printed out? No, they were on his computer. If he wanted them read after his death, had he thought how they might be passed on? Then the penny seemed to drop for him. Who would access the computer when he died? Would his memoirs ever be read? He suddenly asked how he could get them to me, as his printer was not working. I suggested emailing them. Erwin said he did not know how to do this, he had no idea how to send an attachment, but could I talk him through it? Not then though, he said, but the following morning.

It had now been almost a decade after Erwin had first mentioned his memoirs and had then forwarded to me 'Volume 3' detailing his time as a PoW. It was extraordinary that he should now be about to send me 'volumes 1 and 2', recalling his days in Berlin before the war and his years serving in the war.

Seven weeks previously, I had not spoken to Erwin for a very long time. For just a few months leading up to that initial call I had been convinced I would never speak to him again having confirmed that he was a member of one of the most brutal units in the Waffen SS. Would he even want to speak to me if he became convinced that I knew of his unit and its infamy? Additionally, for years I had been sure that even if his memoirs did exist, I would never read them, as I was confident that Anne would destroy them, but now that Anne had predeceased him this threat was no longer present.

The following day, 29 April, I was to receive them. I must admit that I was eager to do so. My excitement mounted. Erwin had mentioned many years before that he would write them down and having had my interest piqued at that time the years passed so the possibility of reading them began to seem increasingly distant if not impossible. However, as the first quiet spring of Covid 2020 stilled our world and caused many to re-evaluate their lives I now felt that Erwin was trusting me greatly. I was conscious of what had brought Erwin to this point of potential handover. His beloved wife had died, the pandemic was at its height, and Erwin felt he had little time left before, as he now often put it, he closed his 'eyes for the last time'. He knew that if he did not act now then his story was likely to go to the grave with him.

I suspected that Anne may have taken much of that story with her, assuming he had told her more than he had committed to his memoirs, there was no way of telling if he had. Now there was just him to tell the tale. However, in his mind he could get me to tell it for him after his own death. I thought this was perhaps his way of ensuring that his account was presented to the world without him having to hear any response to it. The story would be told and there would be no comeback for him, media interest would surely have been significant, after all even then at 98 in 2020 he would have been one of the few remaining German veterans from the Eastern Front.

If I was correct in my thinking, the fact that a former member of the Waffen SS was still alive in the UK would have only added to the interest. Yet, what was it that he had to tell? Why had he kept it secret so long? Had he been involved in something that would incriminate him? The two of us had been much closer geographically more than a decade before, and we hadn't spoken of his PoW days, let alone his war years, for a very long time. It seemed that there was now a race to ensure the safe conveyance of a manuscript that may contain stories and experiences that would garner the attention of many and be of significant historical interest. Who could know how much time Erwin had left? Six weeks had passed since Erwin had taken me by surprise with his phone call shortly before the lockdown, and his own mortality on that occasion had clearly been weighing heavily on his mind. Now, the death rate during the pandemic was increasing daily, especially among the elderly and vulnerable, imminent death seemed a very real possibility.

The next morning, I decided not to show unseemly haste in contacting Erwin. By the time I did so, mid-morning, his carer had arrived and answered the phone. She asked me to ring later, causing me not a little frustration. Nevertheless, I rang at the suggested time. There was a degree of anxiety in Erwin's voice. Was it the fact that he was finally sharing his story with someone else? Or was there another reason? There may have been an element of the former, but he hastily informed me that he could not get on to his emails. How was he going to do this? Was someone able to pop round to help him?

Unfortunately, this not possible due to the restrictions imposed on the nation at that time. Sorting out someone's emails was not viewed as essential. I suggested it might be carried out remotely which was something beyond Erwin's comprehension. Once I explained what this entailed, he understood what I was proposing and Erwin agreed. He was thrilled that I was able to put someone in touch with him to resolve the issue. I contacted Martin, an acquaintance whom I trusted and who owned his own computer business. Within a few hours the manuscript arrived on my pc.

Chapter 10

MEMOIRS VOLUME 1, BERLIN 1922 TO 1941

When I first cast my eyes across Erwin's newly arrived two volumes of memoirs, I quickly discovered that they did indeed cover Erwin's early years and his military service. The latter volume was something I never thought I would ever get the chance to read; but here it was. Several unfamiliar place names came to my attention, some of these would become more familiar two years later in 2023 following the Russian invasion of Ukraine, these included Melitopol and Mariupol. I was to later read published memoirs by other members of the Leibstandarte and find them to be far more detailed than Erwin had recorded, no doubt because they were written some decades earlier and the events easier for them to recall. However, I could not help but wonder whether Erwin had just forgotten the details or if he was simply hiding some of his story. I had no choice but to reflect on what Erwin was prepared to share, and ponder why some periods of time seemed to be missing.

Volume 1 told of his early years in Berlin. His childhood had been difficult. For a long time, he assumed his father's wife was his mother. This illusion was shattered when his older sister, born in 1920 two years before Erwin, disclosed to him one day that their birth mother had died before Erwin had been conscious of her presence. Erwin reckoned that he had probably been around 3 years old when she died. I later discovered that she had died in 1924 just two years after Erwin had been born. Three younger half-siblings were born to this second marriage, two boys and the youngest a girl (Plate 5). His father, Alwyn, was born in 1892; though unemployed he managed to find casual work at the racecourse for which he had to dress up in top hat and tails. When Alwyn was reported, probably by a neighbour reckoned Erwin, to the welfare authorities for working illegally, his response was akin to that which I had grown familiar with. Erwin clearly inherited his father's resourcefulness and wily nature:

> And so father was called to explain what he was up to. And this was his story. 'I was born and grew up in this area and have many friends and old comrades from the army here. There are people dying every day, and with my connections I am being invited to the funerals, which if nothing else provides a free meal for me. What is wrong with that?' With that very plausible explanation, he was let off and if nothing else it made him more careful in the future.

Not only does this account indicate Alwyn's quick thinking, but it also sheds some light on how he may have influenced Erwin's own approach to being in a tricky situation. As we shall see later, Erwin held a profound Christian faith but was pragmatic in that he would do almost anything to survive. Likewise, his father, Alwyn, according to Erwin, was a Salvationist and took his faith very seriously, and yet he clearly had little or no problem in being economical with the truth in order that he retain his unofficial job at the racecourse. Survival was all that mattered in such dire circumstances.

There was clearly a lot of poverty in the Stahlberg family home, as was the case across much of Germany in the 1920s and early 1930s. The household also experienced a poverty in familial relationships.

> Throughout my entire childhood I cannot recall one day when I was alone with my father. On any outing, and they were not that frequent, mother (i.e. step-mother) was always present. I never saw a football-match, or any other sporting event. Matinee shows have been talked about but never visited. Then there were fairs and exhibitions and many other national and international events which I would have liked to be taken to. Apart from all this, there are a number of historical buildings and memorials in the city, which when visited, would have contributed to my general knowledge and history ... The loving relationship between father and son was definitely lacking that personal bonding, and I cannot remember ever hearing father or mother saying 'I love you.'

Much of Erwin's childhood was not dissimilar to many children of his class in Germany at the time: poverty, parental unemployment, a one-off holiday paid for by welfare authorities, and schools that seemed to offer little hope. We should not think of the Depression that followed the Great War as being solely economic, defeat brought about a complete loss of confidence and hope in Germany.

While I was reading Erwin's memoirs during Covid, the biggest pandemic since the Spanish Flu of 1918-1920, I came across Laura Spinney's *Pale Rider, The Spanish Flu of 1918 and how it changed the World.*[vi] I began to realise for the first time how utterly devastating that earlier pandemic had on a world still reeling from the most devastating war in history, even more so on the defeated nation of Germany. I realized the Depression in Germany was caused not just by the aftermath of war, the defeat, and the loss of life, the reparations, and global economic meltdown, especially hard on Germany because of their war debts to the United States, but also by the extraordinary impact and death toll of the influenza outbreak. German society simply did not seem able to recover and return to its pre-Great War heyday. Erwin was growing up in this environment, as were millions of Germans and others across Europe (Plate 6).

According to Erwin's memoirs, Alwyn did not permit Erwin to join any youth movement in the immediate aftermath of Hitler's election in 1933 as he was fully against the Nazi Party. However, on leaving school Erwin states that he had little choice but to join the Hitler Youth:

> When I finished my schooling, my father had arranged for me to start an engineering apprenticeship. This was considered quite a privilege, and as I mentioned earlier, if you want to enjoy privileges, you must conform. I was told quite plainly, 'If you are not a member of the Hitler Youth movement, there would be no apprenticeship for you.' When I confronted my father with this problem, very reluctantly he conceded, and with little time to spare, I became a member.

Curiously, Erwin claimed that he never acquired a Hitler Youth uniform yet was 'seconded to partake in many activities', which seemed extraordinary at the time he made the claim. We shall see later that this was not the case. He gives the impression that belonging to the organisation was less important than the apprenticeship he clearly enjoyed. It was around that time he recalled an incident that introduced him to the existence of concentration camps.

> At 15 to 16 years old, we had formed a group of friends and met regularly and did what boys do. One day one of the gang was missing. Nobody knew what had happened to him. Some time had passed before he was back in the gang. Naturally we asked him 'Where have you been?' When he told us that he was in a concentration camp, we were shocked. 'What

was it like?' we wanted to know. 'If I talk about it, I will be back in tomorrow' was his answer.

On several occasions in the memoirs, Erwin records his concerns about speaking out of turn and the trouble that would have brought upon him. It seemed to me that his writing was clearly an attempt to distance himself from the regime: his father opposing the regime, his father reluctant that Erwin should join a youth organisation, that he only joined the Hitler Youth because he needed an apprenticeship, and his claim that he did not wear the uniform. He also records that when the war broke out, he became concerned about being called up, about food rationing, and about nights spent in shelters during bombing raids.

Alongside these concerns are early examples of Erwin's resourcefulness, a skill he would use to the full later in his life. As a teenager he came to the rescue of a performance in a local cinema where he was working at the time. He had been observing the projectionist for some time, and the work he undertook. On one occasion the projectionist injured his hand, and Erwin was able to step in at the appropriate moment to undertake the next reel change, seamlessly, he said, without the audience noticing any difference, much to the relief of the proprietor.

He described the letter that instructed him to report for military training as 'the dreaded letter'. This came in spring 1941 as Nazi Germany was building its forces up even more for the attack on the Soviet Union in August of that year, Operation Barbarossa.

Interestingly he described the location of the garrison as a 'short journey' from his home 'in a south-western suburb of Berlin'. I had of course already identified that he was a member of the Leibstandarte and that their training centre was at Lichterfelde in the southwest of Berlin. At no point in his memoirs does Erwin mention either.

Not even in the account he wanted me to share after he had 'closed his eyes for the last time' could he admit his membership of the Waffen SS. Was he intending to take this aspect of his service to the grave? Was my role merely to tidy up his grammar and structure so that any future reader would never know of his true military service? This would be impossible. I now knew that anyone could type his name into a search engine and come up with the same result as I had done. It was necessary for me to bide my time before I could confront him with what I knew, and we could hopefully work something out together so that any possible future publication would be open and honest.

Once installed at the barracks, Erwin is proud to record his resourcefulness and ability to quickly learn and adapt:

> Then the time came when we were actually taken to the rifle range to be instructed how to shoot the rifle. By this time I had learned how important it is to listen to every word the instructor tells you. Listening and hearing is one thing, but understanding is more important. All rifles are mass-produced, but that does not mean that that they are all identical. Each rifle has its sights, and it was explained how to line them up with the target to score a perfect hit. In order to explain this in more detail, I like to compare the target with a clock face. When you line up your rifle sight perfectly with the centre of the target, pull the trigger and the shot registered left low about seven o'clock, then you know that in order to hit the centre of the target, you will have to compensate for the error. Sounds a bit complicated, but with a little practice you can achieve perfection.
>
> Because the top achievers were rewarded with a prize I was determined to be at the top. And so my next shot was not aimed at the centre of the target, but at one o'clock right high, and the resulting bull's eye was regarded by the instructor as a lucky shot. When the following shots were equally on or near the centre he changed his mind, and reluctantly admitted 'You are quite a good shot'. My effort was repeated at subsequent rifle range sessions, and this resulted in my name reaching the officers.
>
> When I was told one day to report to the captain's office, I did not know what to expect. Had I been reported for doing something wrong, lots of things went through my mind, because I wanted to be prepared to put up a good defence. When the appointed time came, a knock at the door and in I went, with the proper address, [note that Erwin does not record that the proper address is a *Heil Hitler* salute] and the wave of his hand [again the Hitler salute though apparently in a casual manner] and the friendly look on his face made me realize that it was nothing serious. After asking a few questions about my shooting results, the word reward was mentioned and he handed me a pair of opera tickets, with the permission to be absent on this day. After my thank you I turned on my heels and heard him say as I left, 'There will be more rewards if you keep up the high score.'

After reading the rest of his wartime memoirs and holding subsequent conversations, I found it strange that this recognised skill does not feature again. A marksman not used by the Waffen SS? That was, and remains, a complete mystery to me.

Alongside his resourcefulness Erwin's wily humour could also be gleaned from his memoirs. This humour would also feature on many other occasions later in his life, not least, as we have seen, setting the VE anniversary bonfire alight one night early. Still in the barracks in Berlin:

> Many nights were interrupted by air raids, and that did not go down too well with me. I like my sleep and don't like to be disturbed. The orders were made quite clear to us, as soon as the alarm sounds, everybody, as you are, on the double to the air-raid shelter, which was in the basement. There was no organized meeting point, which made it impossible to check that everybody was accounted for. This made me work out a plan to evade going into the cellar. At the next air raid I put my plan into action. Instead of going to the cellar, I went to the toilet. Sitting quietly, listening to the action outside to die down (NB his comrades heading to the basement) and then back to the room and into bed (NB Whilst everyone else was still sheltering in the basement). Or so I thought, when the door of the toilet opened and someone with a torch shouting, 'anyone here?' As the toilet doors had a ten-inch gap at the bottom, my feet were spotted, the door pushed open and 'out with you on the double'. So much for my plan I thought. There must be a way to overcome this, because I will not give up.
>
> Because the air raids were so frequent, I did not have to wait too long to put plan B into operation. Into the toilet again, but this time I crouched on the seat with feet up and opened the door as much as possible, so that part of the toilet seat was visible. It worked, when the inspector came in and did not see any feet by looking under the door, he left, and I went back to the room into the bunk and had a good night's sleep. Because the return of my mates, after the all clear, was in dribs and drabs, nobody noticed that I had not been out.

While this particular prank has the teenage Erwin desperate to return to bed, the battle-hardened twenty-six-year-old Erwin was more than happy as a PoW to give up his bed in order that he might set fire to the VE anniversary bonfire one night early. Nevertheless, these were good examples of the Erwin whom I knew well, with a twinkle in his eye, a wry smile, and perhaps a chuckle too.

Volume 2 was less humorous, darker, and even though I had looked forward to reading it for such a long time, gave rise to more questions than answers.

Chapter 11

MEMOIRS VOLUME 2, PART 1, MILITARY SERVICE 1941 TO 1942

Once I had read Erwin's memoirs, I searched for any others that may have been written by Leibstandarte veterans. I thought this would be a difficult task. It turned out that it was not the case.

I was surprised to discover that quite a number had been published, both new and second-hand copies were readily available from online booksellers. These tended to have been produced decades after the war. However, one was published in Germany in 1948 and translated into English by Paul Findlay for Collins just three years later in 1951. Erich Kern's account of his experiences in the Leibstandarte, *Dance of Death,* so soon after the war, set out the anti-communist ideology that prevailed in the German psyche, especially so in the Waffen SS. In my opinion, the publisher's anonymous foreword erroneously seeks to justify publication on the grounds that 'one of the most serious consequences of the recent war has been the breakdown of communication between the various peoples of the world.' Despite my belief that poor communication is a significant factor in creating conflict, my view is that there were far more serious consequences of the Second World War than a breakdown in communications.

With the benefit of hindsight and an increased knowledge of the impact of the war, not least from the testimonies of atrocity and Holocaust survivors, the author of the foreword might have wanted to amend their opening sentence. There appears to be a justification for publishing the memoirs because of an underlying fear of Soviet Russia within the foreword, which of course was not uncommon at the time. The foreword goes on to describe the Waffen SS veteran as 'the autobiography of a sincere, if, from a British point of view, confused mind.' It even suggests that the account is 'a remarkable document.' My initial judgment of the foreword developed into recognising that there were indeed good intentions at the heart of the publishers' motives, considering the context, the mind-set, and the social environment of the time. Isn't what I am trying to do in analysing Erwin's memoirs a similar venture? That is creating an understanding of the time? The difference being that I have the benefit of being more critical of his memoirs thanks to many decades of analysis and greater objectivity.

My intention in producing this work is three-fold: firstly, to fulfil Erwin's desire that his experiences be recorded; secondly, to enable a greater understanding of that which leads to a deplorable zeitgeist and utterly destructive outcome; and finally to ensure we ourselves learn from that understanding in order that we might acknowledge our own capacity to inflict great harm on others. All this of course, without providing an apology for the depraved actions of the Nazi movement in all its forms. The foreword to *Dance of Death* probably sums up the likely response for each of the publications: 'Though it may interest many, it may well exasperate more.'

The content of Kern's memoirs made for interesting reading. There is an element of a somewhat sanitised account, but some of the asides were fascinating. Take for example Kern's reference to the hospitality of the Ukrainians, as mentioned by Erwin and referred to earlier:

> For hours on end these south Ukrainian women and children stood in front of the mud houses or lined the road, waving and calling to us: one old woman with trembling hands brought a huge loaf of bread to our car, and was overcome when, with a smile, we refused to accept it.[vii]

I was to discover from Erwin's memoirs that Kern's movements bore a striking resemblance with his, which is not surprising bearing in mind they were both members of the Leibstandarte. The question arose regarding the part Erwin played within it. As we shall come to see, at this point in the war Erwin spent much of this time behind the front at Battalion HQ as a valet or personal assistant to a senior officer, to use his terminology. Nevertheless, Kern's published account does not shy away from some of the dark episodes including an account of a massacre of Soviet prisoners of war.

> At noon next day an order was received by Division to the effect that all prisoners captured during the last three days were to be shot as a reprisal

> for the inhuman atrocities which the Red Army had committed in our sector. It so happened that we had taken very many prisoners during those fatal days and so the lives of four thousand men fell forfeit.[viii]

There follows a pitiful account of men being lined up, eight at a time, by the side of an anti-tank ditch, with the next eight immediately taking the place of the executed men. Kern shows little if no remorse, blaming the plight of the prisoners on their Bolshevik leaders.

Over the course of the next few weeks my internet search history took on quite a change in my usual subject material. Rather than placing an order in the local bookshop I chose to order books online, thus ensuring that those delivering them could not read the titles.

Another memoir *Fűr Volk and Fűrher* published by Helion & Company in 2013 bore a much closer resemblance to Erwin's experiences, albeit more detailed and candid than Erwin ever was with me. Interestingly the author was also named Erwin, Erwin Bartmann. Additionally, Bartmann was also from Berlin and trained at Lichterfelde in 1941 just a few weeks before Erwin. Bartmann too was a PoW in the UK and, again like Erwin, also remained in custody until 1948.

Interestingly, like Erwin, Bartmann sought to hide his membership of the Waffen SS on capture. However, in his case it was not to avoid the attention of his captors but his fellow PoWs. At that stage of the war a sense of denial was widespread amongst the prisoners, the vast majority declaring that they were never members of the NSDAP, that they had an 'utter hatred of Hitler and those old enough vehemently denied ever voting for him. This refutation of their once unshakeable loyalty to the Fűrher – no doubt designed to convince their captors of their innocence of the terrible crimes that the liberation of the concentration camps unearthed – culminated in a vicious vendetta against their fellow prisoners.'[ix]

Bartmann's memoirs go on to describe an incident where the only thing that could identify him as being part of the Leibstandarte was his *soldbuch* (pay book) which fell out of his pocket. A melee ensued as those with him sought to identify the person to whom it belonged. Thankfully for Bartmann he managed to retrieve it and hide it before anyone could link it with him. Interestingly Bartmann, like Erwin in his memoirs, would give thanks to some divine power for rescuing him, in Bartmann's case his 'guardian angel'. Although he recognised that the leadership 'orchestrated monstrous crimes against humanity', Bartmann, like Kern referred to above, was vehemently anti-communist and believed that the war against Soviet Russia was for the greater good. In his concluding remarks he asks what if Hitler had not confronted the threat of communism?[x]

Another memoir by a Leibstandarte veteran that I read was *Obedient to Death* published in German in 2010 and translated into English 2014.[xi] Werner Kindler served throughout the war from beginning to end. Like Erwin, and so many of his comrades, he bitterly complained about the behaviour of Germany's enemies, especially the Russians, who did not abide by the Geneva Convention, which of course they were not signatory to at that time. Russia did not ascribe to the Convention until 1960. Both Kindler and another memoirist Herbert Maeger in *Lost Honour, Betrayed Loyalty* (first published in German in 2002 and translated into English in 2015)[xii] make passing reference to knowledge of mass shootings, albeit briefly in each case:

> In the neighbouring bed was a 30-year-old comrade from a divisional rear unit who had been operated on for appendicitis. He was at first very taciturn and looked depressed. After three days he asked me if he could confide in me and wanted me to answer to swear not to repeat what he was going to say to any other living soul. I gave him my word. He told me that after the capture of a Ukrainian city – as I recall it was Odessa – at the beginning of November 1941 he was ordered with fifty other men of the HQ company of his unit to escort a column of over 3,000 Jewish inhabitants of the city. The walk was eight kilometres to an anti-tank ditch dug by the Russians where he and his colleagues were ordered to shoot the Jews – men, women and children. He confessed that he was deeply troubled by the incident. I was hardly less shocked. Even if previously and never subsequently did I ever hear of such a thing being done by frontline troops or by a rearward unit, from that day onwards after learning of the massacre my critical consciousness grew. And there also grew in me the sense of being threatened by an endlessly huge and inescapable calamity.[xiii]

This paragraph is of particular interest because as we shall see from his own memoirs this was at the time Erwin was in the area and may have been attached to the Leibstandarte HQ to which Maeger refers.

Erwin had always been keen, even from our early conversations to recount what for him was a spiritual experience on the train journey to the Eastern Front. It had troubled me since the first time he had shared it with me verbally, his written account did nothing to alleviate my concerns. It disturbed me because I had difficulty in balancing a member of the SS with a sense of God's presence as he journeyed to the killing fields of Ukraine. However, Erwin's unshakeable confidence in this experience could not be denied. It had become a kind of talisman for Erwin to which he clung during his wartime experiences. It also formed part of his post-war struggle in coming to terms with what he had undergone and witnessed. It may even have eased his survivor's guilt when so many of his comrades had perished. My entire perspective of the Second World War had been that of the Allies and the survivors of Nazi atrocities, so this was a difficult concept for me to wrestle with. However, for Erwin it was clear confirmation that God was present with him as he approached the front.

> What happened next is too important at this stage not to describe in every detail, because it had such a great influence on my future life. During my visits to 'Sunday School' as a boy, I often heard it said, that the 'Lord' will speak to you when the time is right. Perhaps I did not fully understand how this could happen, but on this train journey I had the surprise of my life. There were singing, card games and general jollity, and everyone was in a general relaxed mood, including myself, when I was interrupted in a most unexpected way. The Lord suddenly spoke to me, which made me retreat to a quiet corner, in a most peculiar condition. This is what he said to me – 'Do you know what is in front of you?' I was fully aware who was speaking to me. I had no idea what to expect – 'you will have to shoot and kill people you do not know, and they have done nothing to you,' all I could say in reply – 'I will place my life and my future into your hands and let you guide me.' It took quite some time to recover and compose myself, and I was more than surprised that none of the crowd around me was aware of what had happened. The reassurance, to know that someone is looking after me, is something very special.

For sure, this account is open to interpretation and debate, but it cannot be omitted from my account of our exchanges because it played such an important part in Erwin's mind and his memories of the war years. It could be that the shooting and killing to which Erwin refers in this recollection was a scenario that never materialised, but, as we shall see, that is very difficult to accept. Such possible actions, shooting and killing, may have been playing on Erwin's mind for some time both before and after, as well as in his reflections in later years. How could he justify to himself, a former Sunday school scholar raised in a Salvationist household, what he was about to be part of? Later, how could he justify to himself what he may have witnessed or even done? Yet his account acknowledges that the mood of the train was jolly, card playing, probably scat, a popular game at the time, and singing.

Even Erwin describes himself as relaxed before taken by complete surprise. He was *'interrupted in a most unexpected way.'* The term *'interrupted'* is an interesting choice; it does not indicate a previous concern; it reinforces the term *'unexpected'*. This thought was new to him; he had been doing his duty, training for combat, occasionally seeing it as part of a game, and becoming quite the sharpshooter, an opportunity to impress through his capacity to improvise. This does not sound to me like a man wrestling with angst at facing the enemy in battle. This sounds like a man content with what was before him. Then the reality came home to him as he neared the front, and he began to wonder just what was being asked of him. Even when he was confronted with the possibility of shooting and killing those who had done him no harm, he managed to initiate a justification or a resilience and remained content with his lot based on his experience of being taken by surprise with what he considered to be 'the Lord's voice' addressing him directly. *The reassurance, to know that someone is looking after me, is something very special.* 'The Lord was with me,' as he so often explained his survival. Whatever happened on that train in October 1941, and however he understood it, or others want to interpret it, I can't help but sense the possibility of a tacit admission by Erwin of at least witnessing, if not taking part in something rather sinister. It may be a rare glimpse into the world in which Erwin was operating, a rarity indeed. To this day, I remain unconvinced that Erwin realised what he may well have been disclosing in this account.

I found Heinrich Böll's novel *The Train was on Time* (Penguin Books 2019), originally published in 1949 as *Der Zug war pünktlich,* helpful in imagining the troop train on which Erwin travelled to Ukraine. Böll based his novel on his own experience as a member of the Wehrmacht on a troop train heading east. The cramped conditions, the bravado, the distraction of playing scat, which Erwin recalled are all present.

When I read Erwin's memoirs, it was as if a heavy weight had been lifted from my shoulders. I had been so much in the dark, I had felt some guilt at second guessing what Erwin may have experienced. I felt a degree of shame that I may have been exaggerating in my mind Erwin's involvement. His memoirs of wartime clarified much and allowed me to rest in the knowledge that I was not embellishing what he had experienced. Knowledge really did liberate me.

He recalled the train journey ending in Poland, and after a night in a military barracks was part of a convoy of lorries on a very 'long and uncomfortable drive [that] finished late into the night in Odessa.' He and his colleagues slept on the floor of a cinema with the horses bedded down on straw at the front of the house.

That night Odessa experienced an air raid. The following day the convoy set off again. On arrival at Divisional HQ the newly arrived reinforcements were allocated to their various units. Erwin struck lucky. He was amongst five who were selected to remain with those at HQ. However, because the German advance was rapid Erwin recalled being constantly on the move, entering villages where the houses all contained the symbols of Christianity: icons and candles.

Erwin writes of travelling through Melitopol and on to Taganrog. Indeed, among the photographic negatives he was to later gift me was one taken on a road to Taganrog with a sign stating that the city was 30km ahead and what looks like refugees pushing carts in the distance.

What Erwin does not mention in his accounts are the massacres of Jews, non-Jewish civilians, and Soviet PoWs by the Leibstandarte and the *Einsatzkommando* 10a in Melitopol and Taganrog. I cannot help but conclude that by mentioning these two places Erwin was tacitly acknowledging his presence or at least awareness of what took place there. In his comprehensive biography of Joachim Peiper,[xiv] a senior commander in the Leibstandarte whom we shall encounter again later, Jens Westermeier is clear that members of the Leibstandarte were not only aware of the atrocities but actively participated in the crimes. A total of 1,800 Jews were shot in groups on 25 October 1941 at Petrushina Balka and 8,000 at Taganrog and Mariupol. Westermeier again records that members of the Leibstandarte were responsible, under the command of Peiper.

At some point an incident took place that Erwin would speak of on numerous occasions thereafter both with me and to others:

> It was announced that we were to receive our allowance of alcohol. If that was not a deliberate attempt to deflect or distract from the cold we were suffering, you had better think of a more suitable excuse. There were of course quite a few drinkers looking forward to this event. The way this worked was, one bottle of spirit between so many of us, and one bottle of liquor between so many etc. This meant that in order to get your fair share, someone normally organizes a get together, and who better than the Sgt. Major. When it was arranged to get together for an evening, the venue chosen was the place next to where I was billeted. As I had never been very fond of alcohol, I found it quite easy to decline the invitation to join the party, and thereby forfeiting my share of the booze. Some of my friends could not believe that I prefer a good night's sleep to getting stupid on alcohol. Before I dropped off to sleep, I could hear the loud singing from next door.
>
> What I did not expect, when someone from the party came running into our place, and as I was waking up he was shouting, 'The Sgt. Major shot

Plate 1
Erwin standing next to the Livarot town sign Normandy, 1942.

Plate 2
Erwin having passed his test to drive 10 Tonne vehicles, northern France.

Plate 3
Company with recipient of an award.

Plate 4
Ukrainian women in kitchen. There is no suggestion that these are the women Erwin referred to in his account of villagers providing hospiality and being killed.

Plate 5
Stahlberg family at Christmas,
Erwin is on the right at the front.

Plate 6
Stahlberg children on holiday, Erwin is on the right.

Plate 7
On the road to Taganrog with refugees in the distance.

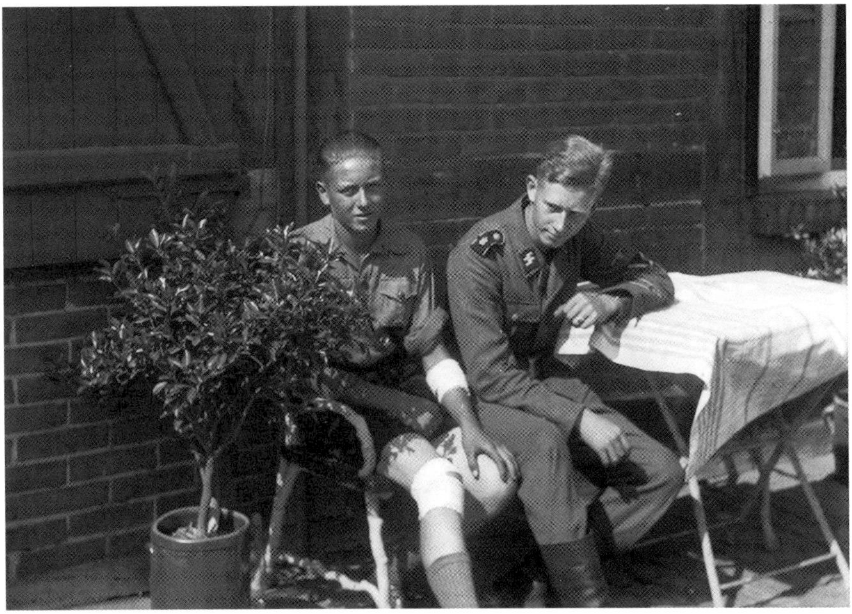

Plate 8
Erwin on leave with injured younger brother in the Hitler Youth.

Plate 9
Firing practice from a distance.

Plate 10
Firing practice close up.

Plate 11
Erwin and comrade with Ukrainian girl and woman, Erwin is on the left.

Plate 12
Troop train passing through Cotbus.

Plate 13
Troop train in Ukraine; Erwin commented on the men sunbathing who failed to duck when the train went under a bridge and were killed.

Plate 14
Erwin's photograph of Joachim Peiper playing cards with his staff.

Plate 15
Close up of what may be Kurt Meyer.

Plate 16
Leibstandarte guard wearing a side arm.

someone dead'. He must have been in shock, when he explained that the Sgt major, in his drunken state wanted to display his 'Wilhelm Tell' trick, when he asked one of the party to stand up against the wall with his drinking beaker on his head, and when he was in position, he pulled his handgun, took aim and pulled the trigger. The bullet hit the poor chap right in the forehead, and he dropped to the floor.

There was nothing I could do, as someone had gone to the captain's quarter to report the tragedy, and he requested that the Sgt. Major be brought to him. The tragic incident went around like wild fire, there was one rather special chap in our squad, who would not disgrace himself with the heavy-weight boxing champion in the ring. I know that he had never liked the Sgt, major, and when he heard the news, he went straight to the place of the incident, grabbed the chap by the scruff of the neck and marched him to the captain. The next day everyone was talking about the incident and the predator was safe in custody

Erwin was incredulous that after a court martial the Sergeant Major (by which Erwin means *SS-Sturmscharfuhrer*) was to be executed by firing squad and the convicted man instructed the squad to get it over and done with quickly because he was feeling cold.

The incident brought Erwin to the attention of the 'judge' whom he called 'Judge S' and Erwin was chosen as his valet:

One day the judge said, 'come with me"' – I had no idea what was happening, and it was not up to me to question the judge. We did not have to walk far, when the reason for our little excursion became apparent to me. We walked right into the main supply depot where all the provisions for the troops are stored. By the manner of the reception we received, I could see that the judge was rather well known for his visits. The officer in charge appeared from somewhere and took the orders from the judge. – A box of cigars, – coffee, – sugar, – and while the officer sent his staff to collect the items, the judge turned to me and said, 'What else do we need?' If I had known what this trip was all about, I would have prepared a shopping list. As it was I just looked at him and said, 'some of us smoked cigarettes, and razor blades and toothpaste is always in short supply'.

No sooner said, and the order was taken care of. Before we left, the judge told the officer that he will not always be coming personally, and requested that I would be his representative. On the way back, I mentioned that if I could have some salt, it would be used as currency for the women who does the laundering, which is always in demand. He just said, 'If we need it, you go and get it'.

I had no intention to abuse it, but it made life at this particular time more tolerable. Before I went on any future 'shopping trips' I always consulted the judge first to get his approval. The day to day activities were carried out with monotonous regularities, and without any news from the front troops.

We were now into 1942 and the weather was getting milder. Where before the roads were impossible to travel because of the snow, the melting made the surface into a thick sticky mess, which made walking almost impossible. At that time the judge had to attend an important meeting in the town, which was not far away, and he knew how he would get there. 'Come with me' was his request, and off we went again. He knew of an artillery unit nearby where he would ask to 'borrow' a horse for the day, so he could ride into town. While the horse was being saddled, he gave me detailed instructions where he was going, and asked me to be there at a certain time to collect the horse and return it to the stable. "Can you ride a horse" he asked, and without hesitation I answered yes. I had no idea what I let myself in for. It appeared that the judge would not return the same day.

So I left on foot to be there at the arranged time. From the direction I was given, it was not difficult to find the place. After identifying myself to the staff, I was taken to the horse, and before I knew it, I was sitting in the saddle. I soon found out, as I was on the way, that there is a lot of difference between sitting on a horse and riding a horse. To my amazement, the horse sensed this right away. Holding the rein, I was told if you pull the right, the horse will go right, and if you pull the left, the horse will go left, or so it should be. If the horse could have spoken to me, this is what I would have heard – 'you can stop this pulling left and right, I know the way back better than you, so just sit tight, and I will get us both back quicker!'

This was proven to me, when without any command from me, he changed from a sedate trot to a gallop, just when we approached a telephone post that had a support strut, and no matter how much I pulled on the rein, he went straight for the support strut, and if I had not laid flat on his back, I would have had a nasty bump on my head. How can I ever forget that ride. I was glad when we reached our destination and I was able to get out of the saddle.

In his account, Erwin lightly passes over the refit in France during 1942 following the Leibstandarte's first tour on the Eastern Front. However, his photographs of that time are numerous and show him and his comrades bathing in the sunshine and standing before what look like significant properties that probably housed the senior officers. It was in France that Erwin took lessons in driving, including large trucks, but this new qualification would bring him into the presence of other significant high-ranking officers.

Chapter 12

MEMOIRS VOLUME 2, PART 2, MILITARY SERVICE 1943 TO 1944

In the autumn of 1942, the Leibstandarte returned to the Eastern Front and Erwin's time as valet to 'Judge S' ended. It was then that Erwin was accused by a 'Captain' (an *SS-Hauptsturmführer*) of stealing some bottles of spirit that he had been transporting:

> I was ordered to see the captain. I had to go and find out, is it something good or bad. When I entered the captains quarters, there was quite a crowd in the room. In the middle was a wooden trunk, which I recognised as having been taken off my truck recently. The captain ask, have you seen this trunk before? of course I said yes, a few day's ago it was of my truck, did you know what was in it?, no, I had no reason to know, well, the captain said, it contained some bottles of spirit, and some of them are missing. 'Are you accusing me of steeling the bottles?' I asked.
>
> Did you ever open the trunk? Was His next question, my answer was no, and I added, that the back of the truck was covered by a canvas cover, supported by some metal strips, and it is not possible to lock securely. That means that anybody could have got at the trunk, especially at night, without leaving any evidence. So I am asking again, are you accusing me of stealing?
>
> Before you answer that question, I would like you to know that I was the valet to the Brigadier Judge 'S' for some time, and was responsible for His meals, drink (some alcohol), and made sure that His clothes were cleaned and ironed, and also made sure that His cigars were always available. On leaving his service, He assured me, that should I ever need His help, I can contact Him freely. I did not have to wait long, when the captain gave a hand signal for me to go. Before I left, I could not go

> before letting the captain know, that if this will have any influence on any possible promotion or granting of home leave, I will have my voice heard.

Clearly 'Brigadier Judge S' was someone to be regarded if not feared even. The identity of 'Judge S' was beginning to make me consider the possibility that Erwin was attached to someone of great significance. When I first asked him, he said he could not remember his name.

In September 1943, in Italy, after the Leibstandarte had been turned back from Rostov and the attempt to relieve the Stalingrad pocket, Erwin was a chauffeur to officers again. He gives few details of his time in northern Italy. Yet there were two significant massacres during his time there: Boves, on 19 September where twenty-three civilians were killed and hundreds of homes destroyed, and a series of massacres around Lake Maggiore in September and October 1943, where fifty-six Jews were killed. Both atrocities again involved Joachim Peiper whom we shall see later is a person of great interest in this account. This silence on the part of Erwin in his memoirs and during our conversations of his time in Italy troubles me.

What Erwin was willing to include in his reminiscences of Italy was that he was again acting as a chauffeur, driving officers to various locations, and delivering documents, presumably orders. He was also keen to include one such trip to Sanremo where he and the young officer he was with, seized the opportunity to enjoy a leisurely drive along the Riviera. One of the photographic negatives he left me appears to be of that day. This part of their journey was of course unauthorised, and Erwin and the officer almost found themselves in trouble:

> Driving south to the Riviera, quite close to Monaco, and from San Remo drove east along the coast, and enjoying our illegal trip in the morning sunshine, when suddenly I spotted in the distance a military check point. I knew that meant trouble, and how to get out of it. As I got closer I could see that the guards were busy checking a very large truck. My thinking was working overtime, and as I got closer, I drove past the checkpoint with no stopping. Why did they let me drive past, I ask myself? Only to see another checkpoint not far away. Now it became clear to me, why I was not stopped. As I stopped, I was asked for my papers, I said, what again, if there is another Checkpoint I might as well stick the papers on the windscreen, there is no need for that he said, if you were checked back there you can go. Further down the road there was a lot of laughing, and I was congratulated on my bold cheek, which saved the day. Now it was time to turn north, and avoid any further checking. I used the country lanes rather than the main roads.

This was Erwin at his roguish best. However, I do not believe his recollection of this unauthorised excursion was to simply provide another example of his mischievousness coupled with his ability to find his way out of a mess. I think it may well have been a hugely significant day for Erwin. He had witnessed the brutality of warfare for almost two years. He had experienced the Russian winter and had become hardened by the sight of death. On this day, under blazing sunshine and the azure, blue sky of the Italian Riviera, with the Ligurian Sea on his left, he may well have experienced a suspension of reality as this brief interlude provided respite from the 'shooting and killing,' to use his term. He will have experienced other days where he and his comrades enjoyed a break in the sunshine, a lengthy refit in France well away from the frontline. Indeed, his photographs show this to be the case with comrades stripped to the waist, wearing the briefest of shorts lying on camp beds in the open, playing cards and drinking; or fraternising with young French women sitting in his Kübelwagen. None of these moments captured in his photographs are mentioned in his memoirs but that day on the Riviera was, it was clearly important for him to recall it.

It reminded me of an episode in Vasily Grossman's *Life and Fate*, one of the finest works of fiction on warfare. The Soviet pilot Lieutenant Viktorov takes a detour following a meeting at HQ and finds himself at the edge of a forest. Seizing the opportunity to take a break from his duties, Viktorov takes a walk through the trees. The beauty of the environment filled his senses: the gentle light on the forest floor; the smell of brushwood, aspen, and elder. As he emerges into a bright glade Viktorov observes lemon-coloured butterflies, and polished, blue-black beetles. He feels the heat of the sun on his metal buttons and belt-clasp.[xv] Though it may not be anywhere near as poetic as Grossman's depiction of course, Erwin's account nonetheless implies that he had experienced something special on the day he too took a detour.

The time in Italy came to an end and after another brutal time in the East the Leibstandarte were relocated to northern France in readiness for the invasion. We know that the Leibstandarte became embroiled in the attempted defence of Caen with significant losses on both sides. It is reported that both the Canadians in their assault and the Leibstandarte gave no quarter. Erwin mentioned to me that because of his earlier time in the region he was very familiar with the roads. It was probably because of this knowledge that he was sent on a mission to retrieve senior officers trapped in a vulnerable position:

At one time a section of our troops was completely surrounded. Because it was known that I had a good knowledge of the locality, and the country lanes, I was chosen to enter at night the enclosed section to rescue some important Officers. The Major, who was my boss at the time, had the information to take out the officers, and was quickly directed to the waiting party.

When they were located, everything was into my little VW jeep type car at top speed, and I was very surprised that the Sgt. Major was also in that group. My heart was beating double time, because I was fully aware of the danger we were facing. The extra weight was making my driving difficult, but a silent prayer for guidance was all that I could rely on. When I reached the end of the enclosure, a military (German) police officer, frantically signalled me to stop, and came closer to tell me to stop the engine, because the cross road is under constant artillery fire, and they go by the sound of vehicle. That prompted the leader of the group to suggest, that they could walk across, and I should follow when given a signal. Before I could gather my thoughts, they were gone, and nobody suggested that they could all have pushed the car across without making any noise.

When I finally was given the signal, I made a formula 1 start and raced across the road, when a sudden explosion on my left side surprised me, but instinct made me race on. I am sure the waiting group was glad that I made it, but before I let them board the car, I got out and inspected that no damage was caused by the explosion. It was no surprise to find the left rear wheel in a damaged situation, and the Sgt. Major was the first to volunteer to help, and asked where the spare wheel is, and when he was told, that is also damaged from an earlier incident, if that did not put him on his high horse of authority and he mentioned that I should be punished for neglect of duty, when the Major (my boss) put him in his place to shut up and get on with the repair, which I was well on the way to complete.

When the journey was completed, one thing was certain, the friendship with the Sgt. Major as down to zero. I was looking for an opportunity to let him know that, when the opportunity came, I was waiting for my boss, when the Sgt. Major came by and asked, if you are going past the kitchen, ask if they have any hamburgers left from last night, to which I said yes. After returning, he was waiting for me and asked, did you ask the kitchen? When I said yes, he was waiting for my answer, what did they say? they said yes, was my answer, it was obvious that he was trying to control his temper. That was one up on me, I thought and our friendship is still zero.

This is no longer a young and inexperienced Erwin, this is a man sure of himself, two tours of the Eastern Front, northern Italy, valet to high-ranking officers, dismissively challenging his Sergeant Major, presumably an *SS-Sturmscharführer.*

Erwin passed over the next months without any reference though the Leibstandarte retreat from France into Belgium was brutal for both sides and the locals. His next entry in his memoirs was of his capture, recorded earlier.

When I read the memoirs of his war years for the first time I could not help but notice that the account of his capture was in far greater detail than Erwin's oral recitation on my first visit to his home in early 2004. It is extraordinary that Erwin survived so much. There are reasons why a German soldier might come through both the Eastern Front and Normandy. Luck had much to do with it, without luck even the most resilient and resourceful of soldiers would not survive so long in a war, especially in the combat zones Erwin had experienced. Erwin had luck, that was for sure, and he was certainly resilient and resourceful, demonstrated by his ability to stem the flow of petrol in the *Kübelwagen* whilst he was still driving under immense pressure after the woman had broken the filter. But there had to be more than luck and resourcefulness to survive so long. Had it something to do with his role? In what capacity had Erwin served? To whom was he attached? Who exactly was 'Brigadier Judge S'? Did the answers to these questions provide a reason for Erwin's survival? I was now keen to follow up on what I had been presented with. All this, however, would have to wait until the restrictions imposed because of Covid were lifted.

Chapter 13

A FACE TO FACE REUNION (AUGUST 2020)

I was travelling home to Lincoln and even the congestion and occasional stationary traffic, so typical of the M5 on a Friday afternoon, could not dampen my spirits. The playlist on Spotify sounded even better than usual. I was in high spirits. The day had gone well, even better than I had hoped for.

Much had changed since I had last visited Erwin in his home. The first being that I had been given the code to a key safe on the wall next to the front door so that I could open it, retrieve the front door key and let myself in because Erwin could no longer get to the door quickly. The code was 1922, the year of his birth, easily remembered.

When I stepped into the bungalow, I immediately noticed something very different: it now had the aura of an elderly man. I turned left into the lounge as I had so often done some years earlier and the first thing that hit me was the space; almost all the furniture had been pushed to the perimeter of the room against the walls.

As I entered, Erwin had his back to me sitting at a table in the front window. He was looking at his red laptop. I could see his body had shrunk with age. There was no Anne, no kettle about to come to the boil, no Welsh cakes recently baked in anticipation of my visit. She was no longer a physical guard standing over Erwin in his chair, as she had so often done in loving protection of the man she clearly adored.

On the journey from a friend's house where I had stayed overnight, I had wondered if I should have telephoned that morning, or better still the day before when I had set off from Lincoln, just to remind him of my visit and ensure that it was still okay for me to do so. What if he had forgotten? What if he was not well? How foolish I was to expect him to be as organised with his diary as he had been when we last met face to face. However, there was no need to have worried. Erwin was still Erwin.

'Hallo Bruce, hallo, come in. Well, well, well.'

He turned and slowly rose to greet me.

He had shrunk, his back was now arched, and he was using a walking frame to correct his balance. However, the eyes were still sparkling, the trimmed moustache could not hide the gentle smile that was so much his own. While his metal framed glasses had given way to a more modern plastic frame there was no mistaking the look of sincere pleasure conveyed through the stronger lenses. I felt humbled to be there and to be greeted so warmly.

Erwin offered me a cup of tea, and I suggested I make one for the two of us, but he had only had breakfast a little while earlier, so he declined. I suggested we have one later.

We sat together at a table in the front window. The table was covered in documents, letters, and files. Much of it was the usual paperwork of someone keeping their daily life together in one place, utility bills, scraps of notes with telephone numbers, and a photograph or two. Erwin soon launched into what he wanted to tell me. It was as if he knew time was of the essence, this could have turned out to be our last face-to-face meeting.

Firstly, he mentioned that he had paperwork, presumably a newspaper clipping because I never managed to see it, claiming that Neville Chamberlain had once said that Prisoners of War were not to come under the Geneva Convention, which appeared to justify the ill treatment that Erwin felt he had experienced in captivity. He then stated that someone at the Nuremberg War Crimes Tribunal had suggested that the Allies were prosecuting Germans for what they themselves had also done.

Secondly, he was keen to share again his memories of his early years in Berlin and his visit to the city in the early 1950s. He recounted how his sister had informed him, when she was 8 and he 6 years old, that the woman he thought of as his mother was in fact their father's second wife, their mother having died before Erwin was conscious of her presence. Erwin wrote that when his mother died his father 'wasted no time to go to his mother-in law, who had quite a large family and asked for the oldest girl to come and look after his two children.'

He spoke with great sadness of his stepmother's lack of affection towards him and his sister, which contrasted greatly with the attention she gave to her own three children, Erwin's two half-brothers, and half-sister. He recalled how his sister disappeared one day without warning. 'When my sister was 15 years old, my father took her by the hand, and without any good-bye or kisses, marched her out of the house and took her somewhere, never to be seen again.'

Once he had managed to get these two things off his chest, it became evident that Erwin wanted to talk about his personal relationships. It was clearly important for him to tell me that he had been married twice. Firstly, to Violet, and secondly to Anne. In the early 1950s, Erwin had become known as 'Mr Fixit' in an area of South Wales that he was living, such was his resourcefulness. There can be no doubt that his skills had been acquired as an apprentice in Berlin, developed later both on the Eastern and Western Fronts, and of course during his time as a PoW. I was under no illusion with regards his abilities and creativity with a presenting problem. At the corner shop near his digs lived M and F. M asked Erwin if he would look at the broken sewing machine that belonged to her sister. When he visited Maud, Violet and Violet's fifteen-year-old daughter were living with her. Having fixed the sewing machine, Violet, or Vi, asked Erwin if he could visit again. Vi was divorced and on 3 April 1954, Erwin's thirty-second birthday, Vi and Erwin married. Vi was ten years his senior. Maud owned the house and expected Erwin and Vi to pay rent. Therefore, Erwin and Vi moved to an empty new house, together with her fifteen-year-old daughter.

One evening on his return from work Erwin found his mother-in-law, whom he called 'Grandma' seated in the house, she had moved in. There was no explanation from Vi. It was just as it was. But this was not good enough for Erwin, he wanted to get away from the wider family that he felt was not taking proper responsibility for his mother-in-law.

He managed to secure a job in Essex, as far away as he could from South Wales. For some time, he and Vi lived apart. After a while, he secured a council house in Essex and Vi and her daughter joined him. But sometime later so did Grandma. This was becoming intolerable for him, so he spoke with his doctor. The doctor made an assessment and felt that Grandma needed to be hospitalised. Shortly after she went into hospital she died. His brothers-in-law collected her body, took it back to Wales and did not invite their sister Vi, her daughter or Erwin to the funeral. The relationship was irrevocably broken.

After a succession of jobs, Erwin heard that some of his colleagues had successfully migrated to the United States for work. Whether he meant his work colleagues or ex-comrades, was not clear. Vi moved with him to the United States.

Thanks to Rebecca, a researcher I engaged to help with the background documentation, she located a record of Erwin's naturalization certificate 9251593, which later came into my possession after Erwin's death. It was dated 3 July 1969, just under three weeks before Neil Armstrong became the first man to walk on the moon. The documentation had Erwin residing at a property in Milford, Connecticut. It seems an idyllic spot and a short walk to the beach, but living in the USA did not work out. One night he came home to find Vi crying, she was homesick, so they decided to return to the UK. I suspect this was 1972 because I have in my possession references from his previous employers in the US: Monarch Die Corporation of Mineola, New York (dated June 21, 1972), and Monarch General again of Mineola, New York (dated August 1, 1972) which had been posted to Erwin and Vi's address in Hove, East Sussex. This could only indicate that he had recently moved back to the UK and was seeking references for a new post.

Later there is another record of him in residence in Nassau, New York. This was after Vi had died and Erwin was remarried; this sojourn remained a mystery to me.

On returning to the UK, Erwin and Vi settled in Hove, East Sussex. In 1971 Erwin spotted a modern block of flats on the sea front which he found much to his liking. He discovered that the flats were owned by Legal & General and that they were mainly occupied by 'Jewish people' (his words). He was not sure what chance he had of securing an apartment, so he spoke to the porter. The porter happened to be Welsh and Erwin thought he warmed to Erwin because of his developing Welsh accent, and, according to Erwin, his surname sounded sufficiently European for the porter to have thought of him as Jewish. The porter 'spoke on (Erwin's) behalf' and Erwin attended an interview in London. He was to live there for thirty years.

Legal & General sold the flats to a property developer who immediately sought to increase the maintenance. When recounting this Erwin smiled and said that as many of the tenants were Jews, they gave the developer a hard time. This antisemitic trope was uncomfortable for me to hear. I was unable to retrieve anything out of Erwin regarding his relationship with his Jewish neighbours.

The flats were again sold by the property developer. Eventually a new owner realised that the best way to make a quick profit was to sell to the tenants. Erwin became the owner of his own home. Vi died and a year later, on 20 August 1993, a neighbour and friend described Erwin being devastated by her death.

Erwin married Anne, whom Erwin had first met forty-three years previously when she was just fifteen, because Anne was Vi's daughter by her first marriage. This fascinated me. Erwin lost his mother when he was so young that he could not recall her. He felt his stepmother had little or no relationship with him. As a young man, and probably later too, he must have felt the loss of a mother-figure in his life. Vi was eleven years his senior and may well have helped fill some of that gap in Erwin's life. Anne happened to be fifteen when he first met her, did he subconsciously see something of his own sister in her? After all she was forced out of the family home at the age of fifteen. What is for sure, Erwin loved them both, and they him. I witnessed at first hand Anne's devotion to him and her protective nature; she hardly left his side in my presence.

Several years passed, and when the block of flats required serious expenditure for two new lifts and refurbishment, Erwin and Anne chose to sell up and move to Wellington, Somerset. It was shortly after they arrived there that they attended the Holocaust Memorial Day event at Queen's College, Taunton at which I was the speaker.

By now, it was time for a comfort break. On my return, Erwin had lifted onto the table at which he was sitting an old brown briefcase that had earlier been on the floor next to his chair. The briefcase, and documents within it were left to me after his death, along with a photo album, which I had previously not known about. The album was to prove a fascinating collection of images relating to Erwin's pre-war and post-captivity years.

As we sat together, Erwin sifted through the documents from the briefcase. He placed one on the table and told me to look at it. Other than a discolouring caused by the passing years it was in pristine condition. It was a small slip of paper folded over and sealed in red with the Nazi eagle and swastika at the centre. Around the eagle were the words *Amtsgericht, Berlin*. 'District Court, Berlin' Erwin informed me. I opened it. Erwin had mentioned this document on the phone when I called to arrange my visit; it was something he very much wanted me to see. It was a certificate, *Beischeinigung,* stating that he was no longer a member of the church. *Diese Bescheinigung ist sorgfaltig aufzubewahren,* this certificate should be kept safe; Erwin had done so for almost eighty years.

It had been signed by Erwin on 4 March 1942, a month before his twentieth birthday. It was post-marked Berlin 5 June 1942. I was only to notice a few days later that on the document Erwin had identified his unit as being SS.

The German State operated what is known as *Kirchensteuer,* a church tax which was placed on all members of the church with the revenue being paid to the church for the upkeep of their buildings. By declaring they were no longer a member of the church a person would not have to pay the church tax. Erwin said that he was ashamed that he had been forced to give up his church membership in this way. This seemed to contradict Erwin's former colleague Bartmann's recollection (referred to earlier). Bartmann recorded that he chose to opt out of church membership with the sole motive of keeping more money in his pocket. Highlighting it as an option, Bartmann recorded that every Catholic in his *Kompanietrupp* chose to retain their membership of the church.[xvi] There was therefore likely no legal requirement for Erwin to do so, unless of course he felt there was no option because he was serving in an environment that was somewhat different to Bartmann, which indeed he was, as a member of staff HQ.

Erwin then invited me to look at his laptop placed on the sideboard that acted as his desk. He was keen for me to see the additions he had made to the last memoir that had been sent to me. I scanned over it. I came to the point where he had written: 'The day came when I said my good-bye, and took the short journey to the garrison, which was in a south-western suburb of Berlin.' Knowing this to be the Leibstandarte barracks, I turned and asked him, 'Was this Lichterfelde?' He did not flinch and there was only the slightest of pauses before he replied with real resolve 'No.' This of course surprised and disappointed me because I knew by then that he was a member of the Leibstandarte, that the Leibstandarte trained at Lichterfelde, and that Lichterfelde was in the south-west suburb of Berlin.

I chose not to challenge him and carried on reading. Erwin said this newly revised account of his life during his active service needed to be sent to me. Perhaps Martin could do this he wondered, just as Martin had helped him some weeks before to send the earlier version. I suggested I do it for him there and then, to which he agreed. The only problem was that it was a very old system, one with which I was wholly unfamiliar. Not being able to see how to attach a file I chose instead to copy and paste the full text into the body of an email and pressed send. Erwin stood over me to watch what I was doing. I checked on my smartphone to see if it had arrived safely in my inbox. On showing Erwin the email on my phone, his face lit up like a youngster at Christmas, 'Well, well, well' and shook his head in astonishment that this could be so easily done, a miracle of modern communication.

Eventually I rose from the seat in front of the laptop and returned to the chair at the table alongside Erwin. I told him that if we were to publish his memoirs the first thing someone would do on seeing his name was to search for him on the internet; and that within a few minutes, they would be able to identify his unit. Erwin sat rigidly still. There was a pause as I let this sink in. I then revealed to him that this was something I had done some months before, probably around the time Anne had died, the timing still fascinating me.

Erwin's eyes did not leave mine. I told him that I had discovered that there were two men with the name Erwin Stahlberg who had served in the German military during the Second World War; one was in the Luftwaffe; the other was in the SS. The one in the SS had been born on 3 April 1922, which I knew to be his birthday. 'The record showed that you were a member of the Leibstandarte.' 'No,' replied Erwin with a serious expression. I must have looked bewildered because a smile then swept across Erwin's face, 'I was in the Leibstandarte.' Erwin had corrected me, Leibstandarte, (pronounced *liebstandarter* with a syllable on the last letter was different to my incorrect pronunciation of *leebstandart*). I could not help but smile too. His mischievous nature that had been so present in most of our conversations over the years, and evident in his memoirs, was alive and well at 98 years of age.

He drove it home after I again stated that his training was at Lichterfelde after all, because this was where the Leibstandarte was based, in the southwest of Berlin, which fitted with Erwin's location in his memoirs. 'No,' he again replied, and with another smile pronounced it correctly for me. I had pronounced it *ick* and not *ish,* it also had a syllable on the last *e* which I had missed off, in other words it was pronounced *Lishterfelder* not *Lickterfeld*. His smile turned into a chuckle, and I joined in with laughter. There was a release in the moment, not just for me, but I think for Erwin too. It had taken more than sixteen years to reach the point that Erwin could finally admit to me that he had served in the SS. We had reached this point without me being too confrontational. The timing seemed right. It felt to me that we may well just be starting afresh with a new-found openness and trust.

I reached for my bag that I had placed next to my chair on arrival. I took out four books. I informed Erwin that I had been doing some reading. I told him that I had come across four memoirs by members of the Leibstandarte. The smile left his face. I took the books out. The covers of the first two showed the SS in action, the third had a photograph of the memoirist, Erwin Bartmann. He took hold of this copy, stared at it, and then placed his forefinger on it. 'He was in my unit. I knew him.' His finger hovered over the badge on the epaulette, the three interwoven letters LAH, Leibstandarte Adolf Hitler.

Erwin stared at me when I told him that I had guessed he had served in the SS sixteen years previously when he had described his capture and the removal of his insignia. Only a member of the SS would do that, I concluded. 'It saved my life,' he said. 'Yes, I know,' I replied, 'many SS prisoners were shot on sight.'

Erwin's eyes went back seventy-six years to that late summer's day in Brussels, his face was rigid while his mouth gave voice to a dark memory, repeating the moment he had come close to being executed. 'Having survived the moment of capture by the Americans I could still have been shot later that night. After I had hidden my pay book in the palliasse, a British soldier came into the cell with a pistol, cocked, finger on the trigger, ready to fire. He shouted out "SS? SS?" He looked around the room, no one moved. He came over to me, ordered me to stand, and stared at me. "SS?" He screamed in my face. "No," I replied and he left the cell. Had I been wearing my insignia I would have been shot.'

It was a solemn moment in our conversation. I told Erwin that I understood that both sides had been brutal around Caen and on occasion no quarter given, no prisoners taken. 'Yes, yes.' His eyes were downcast; his head was shaking slowly. His elbows on the table and both hands, as if in prayer, raised to cover his mouth. Then the silence was broken: 'When we got to Kempton Park racecourse and were being processed the interviewer asked my regiment, I told him I was in an artillery regiment. He told me to take my shirt off and raise my arms. "SS," he said and sent me to join a group of PoWs set apart from the rest, this group were all members of the SS. I couldn't understand how the interviewer had identified them as SS. When I told the others in the group of my surprise, they informed me that only the SS had their blood group tattooed under their upper left arms, apparently the Wehrmacht didn't. I had no idea.'

Erwin then proceeded to do something for which I was wholly unprepared; it was an extraordinary parallel of occasions that I had witnessed previously, a dark irony in fact. He stretched out his left arm, and with his right hand rolled up his shirtsleeve. I had seen others do this before of course; they had revealed a number tattooed on their forearm, survivors of Auschwitz. Erwin's sleeve went higher and under his upper arm was a fading blue tattoo. I think it looked like an *O*, but I was too surprised to fully register the detail. It was an uncanny experience. Without being able to identify them individually my mind suddenly filled with memories of Auschwitz survivors who had revealed the numbers on their arms for the audience they were addressing. I was in the presence of a past very different to that which I had visited on previous occasions. If the documentation on Erwin's desk had not taken me back, nor the admission of being a member of the Leibstandarte, the tattoo certainly had. Not that I had doubted what I had discovered, nor that Erwin's admission had not sunk in, but this somehow placed me, as never before, with him eight decades previously, a teenager forever branded, and forever linked to one of history's most infamous units.

'You see,' he said, 'there are people who would still be interested in me.' I knew this was not one of Erwin's games that he had played for so long, a form of cat and mouse, give a little bit to tease me into thinking there would be more, to hint at a full picture only to reveal a portion of it. It was a truly extraordinary moment. He clearly harboured great fear of being identified. I had no doubt that Erwin had been honest about what he had been prepared to share with me in our previous conversations, limited though it was, but this was the moment the veil was lifted.

I pointed out to him that he would be one of the very last Leibstandarte veterans still alive from their time in Ukraine and Russia in 1941. I suggested there may still be a few from Normandy in 1944 because they would have been younger, but there could not be many remaining of Erwin's cohort, if any. In 2020 the youngest veteran would surely have been aged around 93, for Erwin's cohort no less than 97 years old.

'This is why you can only publish my story after I have closed my eyes for the last time. When that happens, I have left instructions for you to be telephoned straightaway. You must then ring Martin so that he can come and collect the laptop. How he gets it to you is for the two you to arrange.' The seriousness of the moment and the magnitude of the instruction were great. The endgame was nearing. I was going to have to engage in much reflection as time was running out.

I informed Erwin that he might yet outlive me. There may be thirty-seven years between us but one never knows. This did not come as a great surprise to Erwin, but it was clear that a plan B was required. I suggested that if he outlived me then my son should take my place and ensure his memoirs, together with my research and reflections, be published on Erwin's death, but no sooner. Erwin agreed. I then lightened the mood with the comment that I still believed he had every chance of living long enough to receive a telegram from Her Majesty the Queen. Oh, the irony if that were to be the case. This caused us to share another chuckle.

'Well … I never knew you knew so much about me,' commented Erwin. I asked him if I had offended him. His response was without any hesitation whatsoever, certainly not, he was not offended. Indeed, he looked impressed and perhaps had an inkling that I had played a very patient game with him while he had been playing his cat and mouse game with me. Perhaps he thought we had more in common than he had thought. Or perhaps that is why he had chosen to share with me so much, though in tiny snippets of course, over so many years. Perhaps he recognised something of himself in me.

I reiterated how easy it is to now do research on the internet. If Erwin had been naïve about anything then it was because he had not been fully aware of how fast information technology had developed, no fault of someone approaching a hundred years old. I told him that the former Lichterfelde barracks was now one of the sites for the *Bundesarchiv*, Germany's national records office. He looked surprised. I told him that many of the buildings had survived the war. I took out my phone and asked if he would like to see a photo of the place where he had trained. He nodded and when I downloaded an image he moved close to the screen and smiled. His finger slowly and gently touched it and he said, 'yes, yes.' I asked if he could recall the oversized statues of the guards, the 'eternal corporals,' on either side of the entrance, he could. On capturing the area in 1945 the Russians had concreted over them, and the concrete blocks remain to this day. I showed him a photo of the gates with the blocks either side, 'well, well, well.'

I then asked him what I thought was the big question – one that had bothered me since I first saw the abbreviation in his memoirs. Was 'Judge S' in his account Sepp Dietrich? The one whom Erwin had been seconded as a valet. Previously he had said he did not recall the name of 'Judge S.' On this occasion, Erwin responded quickly, 'He was in charge of the Leibstandarte,' he said. 'He was part of the original gang.' His head raised and he seemed to wait for me to follow this up. So, I pressed him for the name of the brigadier to whom he had referred, if it wasn't Dietrich who was it? After all Dietrich was a brigadier. 'I was in the presence of very senior officers,' he replied. 'I did see Dietrich when I was on guard duty one night. I was just outside the toilets when he came out pulling his trousers up. It made me smile that even a man such as this should still be in a compromising position.' I was to later discover that this could not have been the only time Erwin 'saw' Dietrich, but then again Erwin had not said that it was. However, it was clear that this was the end of the conversation for now.

How long had it been since someone had confronted Erwin with the knowledge of the unit in which he had served? Even though we had come a long way over recent weeks, there would always be a great deal that would probably never be addressed. Three years' service in the Leibstandarte SS Adolf Hitler before capture, two tours of the Eastern Front, Italy, Normandy, and Belgium would be a lot to recall. Even so, I doubt the whole story could ever be fully recalled by a 98-year-old man, assuming that he would even want to.

Erwin looked again at the published memoirs on the table before him. He shook his head. I could not discern whether he was shocked at the sight of a known former comrade on the cover of one, or at the fact that someone had shared their story so openly, a kind of betrayal of the SS motto *Meine Ehre Heisst Treue,* My Honour is Loyalty.

Erwin and I parted warmly, despite restrictions on social distancing due to Covid 19 we shook hands and held each other for longer than usual. There was a silence between us. His lips were tight in determination. His eyes were fixed on mine. What was being communicated by Erwin was something I could not detect with certainty. Was he surprised at my discoveries? My new knowledge of him and of his past? Would we ever meet face to face again? Were our conversations drawing to a close? Were we about to reach the concluding chapter of our story?

I drove home with a great sense of relief. As I mentioned at the beginning of this chapter, even the congestion on the M5, typical for a Friday afternoon in August, could not dampen my feelings. For sixteen years, I had not admitted to Erwin that I had guessed he was a member of the SS. I had always assumed he would know that I knew. I could not help but believe that all along he was fully aware of what he was saying to me when he first mentioned the removal of his insignia on being captured in Brussels. Only a member of the SS would have done that. Erwin must surely have known that I would have understood what he was saying. Perhaps it had been our unsaid piece of shared knowledge. However, it had become a burden for me, especially so since the day some months before that I had put in the search engine of my laptop 'Erwin Stahlberg' and found a member of the Leibstandarte SS bearing his name and date of birth. That burden grew heavier as Erwin shared more of his story with me and made me aware of his passionate desire for his memoirs to be published 'after [he had] closed [his] eyes for the last time.'

It was late by the time I arrived home. I slept well. On waking the next morning, I switched on my computer and checked my emails. There was a surprise in store, a shocking one at that. The email that I had sent from Erwin's laptop believing it to be a recent and updated version of his account was there, yes, but as I began to read it, I realised that something was wrong. I had attached the wrong document – it was an even earlier version of the one sent to me some weeks before. The game was clearly not over. I rang Erwin, he laughed at the news. I was again like the young Tommy who had exchanged tins of corned beef for Erwin's watch the day before, only to then discover he still needed the key and had returned in search of the man who had it in his possession.

Chapter 14 (2021)

A ROOM FULL OF ROOMS

Often after I had returned home from a conversation with Erwin, I would take a walk with my dog around nearby lakes, something I also did most mornings and where I could sift through the stream of stuff happening in my life. The picturesque lakes had been formed out of land quarried for stone during the Second World War to construct airfields across Lincolnshire. Even there, within this landscape, where I spent my time relaxing and reflecting, it carried something of the connection with the stories I was hearing. It provided a strong metaphor though – the land that had been scarred and made ugly by the war was now designated a Site of Special Scientific Interest, with flora and fauna in abundance. It was a rural idyll within urban and suburban surroundings. I could watch deer roaming freely, a heron patiently awaiting his next catch, a grass snake scurrying across a path to the safety of the verge, the sun's rays dancing through woodland, and so much more. The transformation from a busy industrial quarry in wartime to a place of great beauty and peace today was clear to see and experience.

It was during one of my walks around the lakes that I realised that even when I was physically present with Erwin, we were not alone, even after Anne's death. I had noticed that at times in the conversations I sensed others with me. My ears were listening to Erwin but my heart was not alone with him. I guess it is possible to say that others were in the room with us because I was still in their rooms. These rooms were where I had sat listening to British veterans and others over the years of my ministry. The front room of a woman in east Manchester who had been a British Army Nurse in northern France in May 1940 telling her story of sitting on a lorry heading for the beaches at Dunkirk only to be shot up by a German Messerschmitt killing many travelling with her. Remarkably she survived unscathed and was part of the miraculous evacuation of 300,000 troops back to the UK.

Also in Manchester, in south Manchester to be precise, I had sat in a man's room when he informed me that he had fled Prague 'after Hitler came.' Of how some time before he left there was a knock at the door late one night. He was in his bedroom, his younger sixteen-year-old sister in hers, when he heard the familiar voices of the parents of another young man speaking to his own parents. They were a wealthy family and had come to announce their departure. They had visas for the UK and that from there they would eventually travel on to the USA. They were to take their son of course, who had fallen in love with the daughter of the household. They were willing to take her too if her parents permitted. They would act as her guardians and if the two teenagers were to marry, they hoped her parents would give her their blessing. However, if she chose not to, they would continue to act as her guardians until her own parents could join them. Her father agreed; her mother did not, saying that they were a family and they would stick together.

The couple left Prague without the sister of the man telling the story. They also managed to reach the UK and eventually the USA where after the war their business thrived. Both families were Jews, only the man telling the story survived from his family.

In a side room at a nursing home in Somerset, I had sat listening to a man with days to live who had been shot down over occupied Europe in 1940. As a trainee architect before the war, he had developed skills that would come in handy, because during his captivity he had time to develop those skills and began to design escape tunnels.

On one occasion the guards guessed there was something amiss and emptied the huts in search of an entrance to a tunnel. They failed to find it, but their suspicions were not allayed. The former RAF PoW laughed when he told me that the guards eventually brought in a ten-ton roller and drove it across the ground outside the huts. The timber support for the tunnel was understandably insufficient for such a weight. In due course, the roller passed over the tunnel below, collapsed it and sank into it several feet. The PoWs were very pleased that the guards struggled for some days to retrieve the roller. I asked the man in which camp he had been held, to which he replied many, because the Germans had realised it would be too risky to leave him for long in any one camp.

On the opposite side of town to the nursing home, I sat with a man who was rightly proud to tell me that he and a colleague had sat in a two-man submarine off the coast of Normandy from the evening of 4 June to the morning of 6 June monitoring the beaches ahead of the largest amphibious assault in history. Of how on the morning of 5

June, the original day scheduled for the landing but postponed due to bad weather, he had popped his periscope up and observed German soldiers playing football on the beach. He joked with his colleague that it would be unlikely the Germans could spend their mornings in this way for much longer.

In the same town I had listened to a man tell his wife's story, because although she was seated with us she was reluctant to do so, such was her humility. Of how she, a WREN, and he, a young naval officer, became engaged to be married and her boss invited him into his office because the boss happened to be Admiral Sir Betram Ramsay. Ramsay was responsible for the naval planning of the D-Day landings, and the woman before me was his personal assistant.

Her now elderly husband spoke of how on Thursday 1 June, he and his young fiancée had evening passes and went together to the cinema; of how at the end of the evening he had suggested to her that they do the same the following Thursday, to which she, knowing that the man before her would be occupied elsewhere a few days later but could not divulge the information, simply replied, 'That would be lovely darling.' As they parted, she knew she may never see her fiancé again, but she had to keep the secret from him.

Her husband continued his account of how five days later at 06.30 hours on Tuesday 6 June the Admiral had led his staff, including his then young fiancée, out of their bunker onto the cliff overlooking the Channel and held a few moments silence as the first US troops stormed the Normandy beaches of Omaha and Utah. At the end of the silence the Admiral told his staff they had to return to their desks because it was going to be a busy day.

A few years earlier I had sat with another man in his room in south Manchester who, at 07.30 hours on 6 June, an hour later than the gathering on the cliff top, was part of the first wave of British and Canadian troops to land on the Normandy beaches. He had sat for the best part of thirty-six hours on a landing craft that was being tossed from side to side in the Solent awaiting the go ahead to set off across a choppy English Channel. He only grasped that this was not one of the drills he had grown accustomed to when the commander of the landing craft told them on embarkation to keep it clean as he would be turning round to collect more lads after he had dropped them off.

Yet here I was often spending time in a room with a man, a veteran of the Eastern Front, who was on the other side of the Channel awaiting to repel the Allies and their attempt to liberate Western Europe. Erwin and I could never be alone in that room, many were with me: they had accompanied me for many years.

So too those who had borne the brunt of Nazi oppression. Those who went into hiding in occupied Netherlands, those who had been transported by cattle truck to concentration camps, those who had seen the smoke rising from the crematoria, and those who had survived against the odds on a Death March. These people would never leave me. And maybe, just maybe, there were others in the room for Erwin too. Perhaps the Ukrainian women who had offered hospitality to him and his comrades, perhaps the Tommy who had fallen for his trick over the watch key, perhaps the guard in the Brussels cell who had threatened to kill him, and perhaps the comrades he had lost, though he never mentioned nor named any one of them as a friend.

It is not possible to know who was in the room with Erwin through his long years of silence, and who accompanied him when he finally began to give an account of his war years. What I can be certain of was that I carried with me the stories of others and often wondered what they would have made of me sitting there listening to a man some would probably have killed during the war years.

Sometimes, but only occasionally, I would just let all this slip by, to accept the burden, to carry the weight of conflicting narratives. There did not seem to be any other course of action open to me. I had gone too far, I had heard too much, my relationship with Erwin too well established, and my pastoral responsibility toward him as valid as any other person with whom I was meeting. Giving of myself in entirety to anyone with whom I was sitting and listening to was my vocational duty, something I could not abandon nor report unless there was the possibility of danger to others in the present or future, and in this instant that was certainly not the case.

Chapter 15

REVELATION (2022)

'That is the Brigadier.'

It took me some days, even weeks, to grasp the enormity of what Erwin was saying. It had been a simple question, and I had not expected a response that would turn the whole relationship on its head. The suspicions of the years dramatically turned into confirmation. Hypothetical possibilities that I had wrestled with for a very long time were finally established. Erwin's usual caution when confronted with evidence that might have resulted in any admission evaporated in a casual recognition as if it were of no importance. Even at the time his words came out it was with such a nonchalance that I quickly moved on to the next slide before I could grasp what he had just divulged. 'That is the Brigadier.'

The second batch of negatives from Erwin had yielded an extraordinary collection of images that included one which would place him at the heart of the Leibstandarte operation in southern Ukraine in 1941/2. It would also locate him at some point in the same room as one the Nazi regime's most notorious war criminals: 'The Brigadier.'

The first batch of negatives he had given me during a conversation in 2021 had been innocuous stuff. Posed photographs of Erwin with comrades relaxing in France, standing in front of a truck having passed his driving test next to an Esso garage in an unidentified town or village. According to Erwin, these were the only negatives still in his possession.

A year or so later, in the summer of 2022, the phone call came that would alert me to what he claimed to be a recently discovered cache of negatives that he 'never knew [he] had.' Erwin was keen to hear when I could collect them. At first, it seemed to me that this was yet another ruse on his part, a way of getting me to journey down to the southwest and meet with him. Nevertheless, I was keen to get hold of the 'newly discovered' negatives, as I could never tell if something would turn into an opportunity to add another piece to the slowly evolving jigsaw of Erwin's wartime service. Time was surely of the essence as well. At this stage of Erwin's life the number of days left were short. Therefore, any documentation still in his possession could easily be lost forever, along with further details of his service. However, opportunities to spend the time driving such a distance, a journey that would keep me from my day job were few, all too few.

Knowing better now how Erwin's mind worked, and how his needs were met, I asked if he would not object to my friend David popping round again and collecting them on my behalf. I recalled that Erwin had enjoyed David's earlier visit and knowing that Erwin trusted him meant that a successful handover could be guaranteed. David collected the negatives within two or three days and was able to bring them to the wedding of my younger son and daughter-in-law shortly after.

The box was five inches square, held shut by two yellow elastic bands. It had once held a recording tape – Scotch Tartan Series – which had first been manufactured in 1960. It was coloured blue across the top half, white at the bottom, with red and blue tartan dividing the two. Erwin's name and address label had been stuck on the top and judging by the condition of the label had been placed there recently. Removing the elastic bands I found within the box four negative wallets, two from France, one from Italy and one from Germany.

Stamped on the French wallets were the developers' addresses: L. Le Saux, 25 Rue Thiers 25, Mantes, Gassicourt, Telephone 761; Opticien Specialiste G. Leroy, 14 Rue Porte-aux- Saints, Mantes. The premises at 14 Rue Porte-aux-Saints remains that of an optician to this day.

Nestled in a row of similarly pre-war buildings, the three-storey building with dormer windows in the loft looks out on a narrow street just off a town square. It was out of this shop that at some point Erwin, almost certainly in SS uniform stepped, holding the Agfa wallet containing his developed negatives. There is no way of telling whether the wallet now in my possession contained the very same negatives, they were almost certainly swopped between various wallets over the years, nevertheless, they provided the evidence that would indicate Erwin had more of a story to tell than he had so far been prepared to share.

Once my friend Paul had digitised the negatives, I arranged to share them with Erwin on Zoom. I was keen to hear what he had to say about some of the photographs that were clearly taken in Ukraine. A grainy image of a make-shift road recently laid with hardcore with what looked like a small group of women, maybe refugees, in the distance, some pushing or pulling a cart; a sign indicated that it was taken 30km from Taganrog (Plate 7).

During the Zoom meeting, when I shared the images with Erwin, he was silent on the photograph. Of course, there is no way of telling when the photograph was taken. What we do know is that the Leibstandarte played a key role alongside the SS Division Wiking in the capture of Taganrog in October 1941 shortly after Erwin and his unit arrived in the region. Anyone suspected of being a member of the Soviet resistance, gypsies, Jews, and communists were shot within days of their capture.

On 22 October Jews were ordered to wear the Star of David. Shortly after they were ordered to report to the Vladimirskaya Plaza at 08.00 hours on the morning of 29 October. They had been falsely informed that due to alleged increasing antisemitism amongst their non-Jewish neighbours they were to be taken to a ghetto for their safety. All Jews and those married to Jews were expected to gather. They were told to bring the keys to their accommodation with a label stating the address. It was recommended that they carry with them all their valuables and cash.

Once they had all gathered, they were taken by trucks to a gully where they were shot to death by Ukrainian collaborationist auxiliary police under the direction of the Einsatzgruppen, the SS paramilitary death squads. In all 2,500 Jews were massacred on that day, with just one teenage boy surviving thanks to the protection of non-Jewish Ukrainian helpers.

The cache of negatives recorded several places where Erwin was during the war years. What excited Erwin most was seeing himself on leave photographed alongside his brother. Erwin was in uniform, his half-brother in the uniform of the Hitler Youth. The latter had his right leg and left arm bandaged due to an accident on the farm where he had been working (Plate 8).

I was keen to get back to even more intriguing images. Three were of what appeared to be some form of training. The first was taken of what looked like a back garden from a distance, high up, maybe from the bedroom window of a house.

Nine soldiers are gathered in a group to the right of the photograph, to the left at about 12 yards from the group is an officer appearing to address them. Close to him is a soldier seated at a small table serving as a desk, three others, one of whom is carrying a rifle, and another who is lying face down (Plate 9).

A second photograph is clearly taken closer to the group (Plate 10). The officer is still speaking but appears to have been taken by surprise by the photographer, presumably Erwin. The three soldiers around the officer are nonplussed and the one at the desk can only be partially seen. A third photograph, almost certainly from the same location, is of soldiers firing a machine gun with others standing near looking through binoculars. I asked Erwin what the photographs were of and he responded, 'I couldn't say, practice perhaps, maybe for an execution.' It was an extraordinary comment, though I could not believe the photographs were of Leibstandarte soldiers practising for an execution, to me it seemed a regular shooting practice, and yet it is not possible to know for sure. What is for sure was Erwin's extraordinary response.

There were many photographs in the cache of Erwin and his comrades resting and sunbathing. None of these amounted to much other than the extraordinary youthfulness of some of them. Stripped of their SS uniform with just a pair of exercise shorts or swimming trunks some appeared nothing like a force to be reckoned with, certainly not what I would have imagined Hitler's elite to be. They were far from propaganda poster boys for the Aryan race. However, a few were clearly characters who appeared to match the image many of us have formed of the SS.

Two photographs of Erwin (Plate 11) with a comrade sitting with what looked like a Ukrainian woman and her teenage daughter brought recognition from Erwin. 'Ah yes, I remember this being taken.' The woman, teenager, and colleague are seated together on a bench; Erwin has perched himself on the back of the bench behind the woman. He looks happy with himself. Was this the woman that had asked Erwin to make her daughter pregnant so that she would not be sent to Germany as part of the labour 'recruitment'? It is not something that Erwin would divulge. I could not help but feel there was something unpleasant about Erwin recounting this request. Then again, I must remember that I am judging the request from a very different time and position to that of the woman. Over the course of history, what have people been prepared to do to save their loved ones or themselves? In times of war, and out of desperation, people have often amended their bar of morality to survive.

One photograph was taken from a troop train passing through a station (Plate 12). The sign above a platform indicates that it is Cottbus, the industrial city in south-eastern Germany, approximately halfway between Dresden and Berlin. It is an extraordinary image capturing a moment in time. The platform is busy, soldiers milling around, one an officer, with his bicycle and an attaché case. There is a blond-haired schoolboy in shorts, women chatting to an older man, on a far platform people boarding a waiting train. The troop train has clearly passed through a wooded area because oak leaves have been caught in the steel frame of one of the trucks. It may be that this was taken on the withdrawal from the Eastern Front as the Leibstandarte made their way to France for a refit in the summer of 1942.

Amongst the collection of newly digitised photographs were a significant number taken during that refit. These were of interest to Erwin, but none provoked the response that one from a troop train did. (Plate 13) This was taken in southern Ukraine around what looks like either the Black Sea or the Sea of Azov.

On first sight I had found the photograph extraordinary. It captured a moment in time filled with story. The train was of course pulled by a steam locomotive which is clearly visible in the top right corner of the photograph. In addition, there are buildings in the top left, one damaged, perhaps because of military action, but it is difficult to be sure. The sea or an estuary is beyond those buildings, and in front of the buildings heading towards the foreground are three men on a cart pulled by a horse. Each is wearing a *kenka,* which resembles what we in Britain might think of as a Guernsey fishing cap. Two are facing forwards, the third, at the back is sitting side on with his head down. What is their story? Where have they been? Where are they going?

None of these details were of interest to Erwin. Something else in the image caught his eye and sparked his memory. On seeing the image, he immediately lent forward towards the screen, peered at it, and laughed a little.

'Ah,' he began. 'You see those men? On the trucks without their shirts on? They were sunbathing; but when we went under a bridge they forgot to duck; they got killed.'

Erwin said it with a flippancy that shocked me.

It reminded me of a throw away comment from a conversation we had a year or so before. We had chatted about the battle for Caen in June 1944, where the Leibstandarte had helped hold up the Canadian and British advance. As mentioned previously, I had read that it was particularly bloody with little quarter given on either side.

I asked him what it had been like, bearing in mind the number of deaths he must have witnessed. Again, his response was without emotion, a wholly unguarded moment, 'Oh by then I was used to dead bodies. You must remember that I had already become quite an expert on making the most of the space on the back of a lorry by packing bodies in a certain way.' I recalled that a term had been coined by the Nazis to describe such a method of packing bodies closely together in mass graves after an atrocity: *Sardinenpackung*. Few will need a translation.

A chill went through me. In the near twenty years I had known him, he had never been so explicit, nor so dismissive of what he had witnessed. So shocked was I that I could not follow it up with him, and I regret not doing so. When? Where? What bodies? Comrades? Russians? British? Canadians? Civilians? Jews?

Twice now, in our recent conversations, Erwin had been dismissive about death. This was far from the Erwin that had voiced regret at the hospitality of Ukrainian women who had invited him and his comrades into their home and offered them food and drink. When recounting this latter incident, he had shaken his head in shock and remorse saying that he could not understand why they would do this when they must have known 'we had come to kill them.' On that occasion, I had wondered whether he was referring to killing these women specifically or speaking in more general terms about their fellow Ukrainians fighting the Nazi invaders. The casualness with which he then spoke of making the best use of space when packing bodies on lorries, and now acting so dismissively at his own comrades' needless deaths on board a troop train, possibly heading for France and some respite, led me to consider the very real possibility that he had meant the women themselves were to be killed, and maybe others.

Was he admitting that he was directly involved? On the other hand, was the term 'we' a more collective acknowledgment? That is 'we' being the Nazi regime or Leibstandarte? If I had asked him at that point which it was, I do not think I would have got a clear and unequivocal answer, especially had it been the former. However, despite all this, I still could not see the man before me as someone who would take the lives of unarmed civilians so willingly. It just did not fit with the gentle, caring person I had come to know; but war is war and many decades had passed since.

I had met at least two killers in my role as assistant police chaplain early on in my ministry. I had been invited by the station to visit them in their respective cells shortly after they had been arrested. One was deemed a serial killer by the sergeant having randomly taken the lives of three women. Sitting with him in his cell was an unforgettable experience. He sat on his bed so tightly wound up in a foetal position I felt it might be possible to cause him to roll had I touched him. He did not move once or speak one word in the time I sat with him, a still silence that begged the question how human this person was.

The second experience was altogether different. This man had beaten his girlfriend to death, yet he spoke with me as if he had been brought in for a minor traffic offence, and unjustly so at that. Several times during our conversation, he gently requested I ask the police, on his behalf, permission to attend his late girlfriend's funeral. I found different ways of saying that this was not my role nor in my brief. The conversation was all so natural and rational, until he finally got the message that I really wasn't going to do as he asked – he turned and looked at me in such a way that I had not seen before or since. His demeanour switched in a flash from someone with whom one would be happy to have a drink in the local pub, to someone altogether different, leaving me in no doubt that this was a man who could clearly kill given the chance. Erwin was neither of these men.

The next photograph that I showed Erwin changed everything for me (Plate 14). I had deliberately kept it until late on in my presentation of images. Five relaxed men sitting round a table, playing cards, one keeping a scorecard while another, an officer, with a large cigar in his mouth, about to play his hand. Those facing the camera have their shirts unbuttoned, including the officer. His epaulettes indicate that he was of senior rank. Rifles are propped up in the corner behind him and what looks like a towel is covering what may be the window, blacking it out. 'What rank is the officer, Erwin?' Without any hesitation he replied, 'that is the Brigadier.'

Chapter 16

ADMISSIONS

Only once does Erwin use the term 'Brigadier' in his memoirs. He recounts an episode where he was accused by a captain of helping himself to some booty that he had been asked to deliver. Even though Erwin pleaded his innocence, it became clear that the captain did not believe him. As a last resort, he named the brigadier, for whom he had served as his valet.

> I was the valet to the Brigadier for some time, and was responsible for his meals, drink (some alcohol), and made sure that his clothes were cleaned and ironed, and also made sure that his cigars were always available. On leaving his service, He assured me, that should I ever need his help, I can (sic) contact him freely.

The identity of the senior officer to whom Erwin was allocated had been a topic of conversation between us as soon as I had read his memoirs. In the initial version he had often referred to him as 'Judge S' which is why I had long suspected him to have been *Oberstgruppenführer* Josef Dietrich. Josef was shortened to 'Sepp' and his men fondly referred to him as 'Sepp.' Could Judge S have been Sepp Dietrich, head of the Leibstandarte since its conception, and very close to Hitler?

When I confronted Erwin with the possibility he hastily and forcefully denied it. Within a few weeks an updated version of the memoirs arrived. In this new edition the references to the senior officer were now only as 'Judge,' the 'S' had suddenly disappeared. For me this was tacit confirmation that Erwin had at some point served Dietrich as his valet. Dietrich had long fancied himself as a cavalry officer but a broken leg earlier in his life had ended his ambition in that area and the following extract from Erwin's memoirs is intriguing as well as humorous:

> Where before the roads were impossible to travel because of the snow, the melting made the surface into a thick sticky mess, which made walking almost impossible. At that time the judge had to attend an important meeting in the town, which was not far away, and he knew how he would get there. – 'Come with me' was his request, and off we went again. He knew of an artillery unit nearby where he would ask to 'borrow' a horse for the day, so he could ride into town.
>
> While the horse was being saddled, he gave me detailed instructions where he was going, and asked me to be there at a certain time to collect the horse and return it to the stable. 'Can you ride a horse' he asked, and without hesitation I answered yes. I had no idea what I let myself in for. It appeared that the judge would not return the same day. So I left on foot to be there at the arranged time.
>
> From the direction I was given, it was not difficult to find the place. After identifying myself to the staff, I was taken to the horse, and before I knew it, I was sitting in the saddle. I soon found out, as I was on the way, that there is a lot of difference between sitting on a horse and riding a horse. To my amazement, the horse sensed this right away. Holding the rein, I was told if you pull the right, the horse will go right, and if you pull the left, the horse will go left, or so it should be. If the horse could have spoken to me, this is what I would have heard –
>
> 'you can stop this pulling left and right, I know the way back better than you, so just sit tight, and I will get us both back quicker'! This was proven to me, when without any command from me, he changed from a sedate trot to a gallop, just when we approached a telephone post that had a support strut, and no matter how much I pulled on the rein, he went straight for the support strut, and if I had not laid flat on his back, I would have had a nasty bump on my head. How can I ever forget that ride. I was glad when we reached our destination and I was able to get out of the saddle.

Whether the brigadier to whom Erwin was referring as he recounted the incident of the missing booty and the threat to call on his former boss was Dietrich or someone else is simply not possible to prove. However, what is fascinating is that in the newly revised edition of his memoirs the incident with the horse had been removed. My question about the identity of the senior officer had clearly made Erwin uncomfortable, especially perhaps because I had mentioned that I understood Dietrich liked horses.

Returning to the image of the senior officer and his men playing cards I asked Erwin what the rank of the officer was, he had no hesitation in say 'Oh that is the Brigadier.' After our conversation I immediately looked up the uniforms of the SS. I discovered that the uniform in the photograph was not that of a brigadier. The insignia on the shoulder indicated an *Obersturmbannführer* (lieutenant colonel). I looked up Leibstandarte *Obersturmbannführers* and came up with the name of Joachim or 'Jochen' Peiper. It did not take long to compare archive images of Peiper with Erwin's photograph, there was no doubt about it: Erwin was part of Peiper's staff.

Placing Erwin in the room with Joachim Peiper changed the whole dynamic of the relationship between Erwin and myself. Up until then I had allowed much of my understanding to be forged by Erwin's own account of his wartime experiences. Yes, I remained somewhat sceptical, as I could be no other. After all, I was not going to allow my openness and willingness to lead me to believe in any form of revisionism. The facts spoke for themselves.

Of course he had been in the Hitler Youth, that was a given. From the outset, he readily admitted he had acted as chauffeur or even adjutant to a senior officer. He had even been involved in carrying loot for a senior officer. I knew that he had served on the eastern front. Yes, he was someone who claimed to have not known anything at the time when I asked him about the Holocaust, and regardless of my doubts, I had always taken his response to be plausible if it meant the possibility that he was referring to Auschwitz and the other death camps, rather than the 'Holocaust by bullets' on the Eastern Front. Such denial was common amongst wartime Germans despite evidence to the contrary. After a few years of course, Erwin had to admit that he was a member of Hitler's SS, the Leibstandarte no less – something he had sought to initially hide from his captors and subsequently almost everyone else perhaps. Once I knew that he had been a member of the Leibstandarte I researched their founding, their evolvement, their activities, and the atrocities attributed to them. I also came to see that they had suffered huge losses in the Ukraine and Russia campaigns of 1941/2 and 1943.

For someone to enter the Leibstandarte in the spring of 1941 and survive the entire war was rare. Erwin was one such person. Not only that, of course, but he had lived to an extraordinary age. There could not be many Leibstandarte veterans still alive in 2023 let alone those that had been recruited as early as 1941. In my own mind Erwin surely could not have gone through his service without noticing the massacre of Jews or the massacre of Soviet prisoners of war.

Although there is some debate about the exact numbers, it is often claimed that 10,000 Soviet PoWs were executed by the Leibstandarte in October 1941, the month Erwin arrived at the front. At the very least, even had he not been in the immediate vicinity of the atrocities, surely, he could not possibly have ignored the gossip or first-hand accounts of atrocities, they were too prevalent and involved too many people.

In one conversation I broached the subject again, this time with greater confidence because of my new-found knowledge.

'So, Erwin, the guys that carried out the killings, were they always the same guys or were they randomly chosen?'

'Usually the same ones.'

'Did they talk about it or keep it to themselves?'

'Oh, some were boastful. They always wanted others to know how many they had killed.'

'And did they drink alcohol before they went out and do this? I have read that they were plied with alcohol."'

'No, goodness no, they had to be sober. They drank heavily afterwards.'

In the earlier years Erwin had possibly hinted at his experience of killings when he had admitted that he felt guilty about receiving hospitality from those they had come to kill. The admission was still ambiguous though. It was not specific and he may have been referring to the killing of the men of Ukraine or Russia in battle. However, a part of me always felt it was a glimpse into something far more sinister. Now though, placing him in the room with Peiper puts him in direct contact with one of the most notorious of Nazi war criminals.

Joachim Peiper, or 'Jochen' as he preferred to be known as, was the rising star of the Waffen SS. He was young, dashing, and intensely loyal. Peiper was a favourite of none other than Heinrich Himmler, Reichsführer of the SS.

He was born in Berlin in 1915. He and his two brothers were raised in a bourgeois home protected from the unrest and poverty that afflicted so much of Germany in the 1920s.[xvii] The father often reminisced about his time as an officer in the Imperial Prussian Army in Africa. Joachim soon declared his intention to join the military.

As a teenager, he watched the street protests between the various factions of German politics. Under the influence of their nationalist father, it is hardly surprising that Joachim and his brother Horst joined the Hitlerjugend in the spring of 1933, before it became compulsory. By October 1933 Joachim was a member of the SS. Their brother Hans-Hasso was by then in a vegetative state having attempted suicide owing to his homosexuality. Hans-Hasso was later murdered under the euthanasia programme by the Nazi regime.

Peiper's rise through the ranks was meteoric. He impressed his seniors and in September 1934 caught the eye of the head of the SS Heinrich Himmler. Four months later Peiper was on a Leibstandarte Leaders' course, only possible through the personal support of Himmler and head of the Leibstandarte Sepp Dietrich.

Military ambition was not the only thing propelling Peiper, his political worldview had now been formed, he was a true believer in the Nazi cause. Three years later, in 1938, the 23-year-old joined Himmler's personal staff and became his first adjutant in the summer of 1939. Alongside Himmler, Peiper was fully aware of the concentration camp system and the intentions of the Nazi regime. He experienced some of the camps at first hand and felt no remorse, quite the contrary. He also visited Poland in 1939 and alongside Himmler observed the so-called 'Jewish problem.'

Peiper's first taste of front-line combat came in France in the summer of 1940 where he may have suffered minor wounds. Himmler quickly ordered his return to the staff HQ. Following the initial success of Operation *Barbarossa,* the attack on the Soviet Union in June 1941, vast numbers of Jews fell into the hands of the Nazi regime. It was not long before the aspirations of the Nazis coupled with the deep-seated hostility of locals towards their Jewish neighbours could turn into a dark reality. The randomness of the killings became an issue for the Nazi hierarchy, and they began to make plans for a more organised method of conducting massacres on an industrial scale.

In the full knowledge of Himmler's wishes and intentions Peiper travelled to the south of Ukraine when a new contingent of the Leibstandarte arrived there fresh from Germany in October 1941. Erwin was part of that contingent. They had been sent to replenish the depleted forces that had taken part in the initial assault over the summer. Very shortly afterwards the Leibstandarte carried out massacres of Jewish civilians in various areas that they occupied.

It has often been argued by members of the Waffen SS, and their apologists, that the massacres were the sole responsibility of the Einsatzgruppen, the special unit set aside for the killing of mass numbers of Jews and others behind the front lines. Thus, the Waffen SS, such as the Leibstandarte, were often able to deflect criticism and deny charges of culpability. However, members of the Leibstandarte not only took part in the rounding up of Jews and other civilians but were also guilty of participating in the murders.

Jens Westemeier in his critical and deeply researched biography of Peiper is quite clear in his conclusion that no member of the Leibstandarte could possibly have not known about the atrocities, not just of Jewish civilians but also of Soviet prisoners of war. Peiper may well have been one of Heinrich Himmler's senior operatives in seeking to erase Jews and other *Untermensch* (racially or socially inferior) across Eastern Europe.

Peiper was popular both among his superiors, especially Himmler of course, and amongst the men under his command. In addition, his wife Sigurd was a childhood friend of the woman who married Himmler's deputy, Reinhard Heydrich. In the post-war years Nazi sympathisers would continue to hold Peiper up as an icon of the fascist regime.

Peiper was responsible for several war crimes. He was in command of the Leibstandarte in northern Italy when it carried out a massacre of civilians at Boves, on 19 September 1943, just eleven days after the Italians had capitulated. A German soldier had been killed and two NCOs taken captive by Italian partisans near the town. Peiper negotiated the release of the NCOs and promised that the town would be spared. He did not keep his word. In all twenty-three civilians were killed and the town destroyed by Leibstandarte artillery.

Peiper was also ultimately responsible for the massacre of American GIs at Malmedy during the Battle of the Bulge. These were the atrocities for which he stood trial for war crimes, but they were not isolated events.

In July 1946 Peiper was sentenced to death by hanging following a trial investigating the Malmedy massacre. The sentence was commuted to thirty-five years imprisonment and he was released in 1956. After his release he obtained some work in West Germany but eventually set up home in France where in 1976 he was recognised and was assassinated by what may have been former French Resistance or communists.

The question for us then is not necessarily the actions of Peiper but of Erwin's knowledge and potential collaboration or complicity. This new twist in my relationship with Erwin was a significant one. There is a sense in which had Erwin acknowledged these actions that took place, and the tragic crimes that were committed, then I think I would have less problem in believing that he had absolutely nothing to do with it. But the fact that he could not even admit these events took place, and that he claimed he had no idea of them at all remains deeply worrying. Additionally, I had once asked Erwin if he was conscripted or if he had volunteered, and he very quickly responded that he had been conscripted. I found this hard to believe and I later discovered that conscripts were only admitted to the Leibstandarte after huge losses in the winter of 1943, a full two and a half years after Erwin had joined the Leibstandarte. It was only then that the requirements for racial purity and loyalty to the ideology were eased.

PART III
REFLECTIONS

Chapter 17

GETTING CLOSER TO THE TRUTH

None of this research and exposure to the thinking and actions of the Leibstandarte altered my own convictions about the Holocaust, nor did it diminish my commitment to raising awareness of the Jew-hatred that led to it. Far from it. If anything, I found that my resolve to challenge the centuries-old prejudices that had seen Jews massacred at regular intervals across Europe and stand up to its resurgence in my own time and place doubled. Erwin's experience and his undoubtedly profound faith was teaching me much about the ease with which we can all be swept along by an attractive ideology, one that promises escape from poverty, provides a sense of dignity, and not least a sense of belonging and purpose.

While my own encounters with the history of the Second World War through reading, TV documentaries in childhood and teenage years, and through conversations in adulthood with British veterans, those on the Home Front, and above all else Holocaust survivors, remained the bedrock of my commitment, my knowledge of Erwin and his story was an additional driving force. I gave much time and energy to writing my book *Echoes of Contempt – a history of Judeophobia on the Christian Church,* which was published in 2018, in other words before it was confirmed that Erwin had been a member of the SS. Although Erwin of course is not mentioned in the book by name, the impact he had on my thinking was very much present.

Several of the stories he shared with me were anonymously referenced in a chapter that reflected on the Holocaust and how it came about in such a deeply sophisticated Christian country – the election of Hitler, the banners and spring flowers post-election, the newly-restored pride, the hospitality of Ukrainian villagers who may have been targeted for killing, and the removal of his insignia on capture. I concluded the paragraph with the following:

> Sitting with someone who was so likable, a proud Christian who was devoted to the study of Scripture, brought home to me the very real possibility that I might not have been a rescuer, nor a bystander, but a perpetrator.[xviii]

Among others, Erwin was also a reason for my passion in challenging antisemitism wherever I believed it was forming. I recognised in him and his story that any one of us could become complicit in what is known as 'the longest hatred,' no matter how good and noble our intentions. Indeed, through my research, I discovered the role the Methodist Church in Germany played in supporting Hitler and the Nazi movement. From the very top to members in local churches, Methodists tended to be at least compliant if not avid supporters. As a Methodist minister in the UK decades after the war, I was horrified at both this new-found knowledge and equally horrified to discover letters published in the weekly newspaper, the *Methodist Recorder*, from the 1930s that sought to justify the actions of the Nazis in Germany.

I began to more strongly feel that only honesty about our past and a humility in the present were the proper recourses to what I was learning. More honesty would lead to greater humility, and more humility to greater honesty, virtues that seem to be in retreat in our world today.

The longer I had with Erwin the greater the opportunity I had to learn, not only of him but also of me, not only of what it was like to be drawn into a sinister ideology but also of the threat obsessive beliefs present in our world today. Despite the extraordinary conversations we were holding, and my own heightened awareness of the perils of extremist philosophies and activism, there was never any question of me breaking the confidentiality of our encounters. I would continually wrestle with what Erwin saw in me: a confessing figure, a priest and pastor, the son he never related to, or something else. However, what I was sure of was the value of learning more about human nature, living under a dictatorship, and living with events over which someone has little or no control.

After having shared the developed photographic negatives with Erwin in an on-line chat we agreed to meet in person so that he could see them properly. I felt this would be very different to the previous occasions we had chatted either online or in person. I felt a sense of anticipation. There was an element of confrontation as well as disclosure, revelation, and encounter. I could not dismiss the fact that this felt like it was going to be a significant occasion. This would be the moment I was to see Erwin's reaction to the fact that I knew he was in the same room as Joachim Peiper, convicted war criminal, adjutant to Himmler, thoroughly nasty individual. Nevertheless, I had for some time been mindful of Erwin's increasing frailty and was cautious about causing him undue distress which might have led to a serious deterioration in his health, for which I would have rightly felt culpable.

When I had previously shared the somewhat damning image with Erwin on our call, he had instantly declared the senior officer as 'the Brigadier', no hesitation, utterly convinced of the identity of the cigar-smoking man sat at complete ease around a table with his very relaxed underlings. Having heard over the years Erwin himself recount incidents with the Brigadier and read in more detail in his memoirs of the Brigadier, I could not help but consider that the officer whom Erwin had photographed that day was in fact the one and same 'Brigadier' to whom he had referred.

It was only after the initial call that I double-checked the rank of the officer from his right shoulder and discovered him to be an *Obersturmbannführer*. Then through a simple search of senior Leibstandarte officers I matched the officer in the room with *Obersturmbannführer* Joachim 'Jochen' Peiper. At first, I thought the image was from Ukraine. Peiper had been sent to Ukraine at the same time as Erwin had been, October 1941. It stood to reason that on arrival Peiper would have needed a team around him that would provide for his needs, and Erwin had been selected as one of those that would act as chauffer and 'valet', to use Erwin's words.

The killing of Jews in that area commenced at that time, possibly because Peiper carried to the sector the unwritten orders from his boss Himmler. The Leibstandarte did not wait for the Einsatzgruppen to arrive, the unit that was attached to the Waffen SS but set apart for mass killing. The Leibstandarte were fully involved in the rounding up and shooting of Jews during October 1941.

The photograph that Erwin took looked as if it was at the end of the day, the men looked as if they had been busy. Peiper's tunic was unbuttoned, the man to his left was stripped to his undershirt, and there were rifles in the corner. Was the photograph taken in Ukraine? This possibility troubled me for several months, had Erwin been part of a group that had taken part in the killings? It had led me to ask him if the same men took part in the shootings each time or if they were constantly changed. As I reported earlier Erwin did not have to consider his response, nor dig deep into his memory: 'Usually the same ones,' and went on to say that they were boastful of the numbers they had killed. It had been a remarkably lucid and candid admission on the part of Erwin. I had not misheard him, there was no reason to doubt him, and I had not exaggerated in my mind what he had said. However, after further investigation, I was to discover that the photograph was not taken in Ukraine after all, most likely France because Peiper was not promoted to *Obersturmbannführer* until January 1944. The photograph was almost certainly taken in the lead up to the Allied invasion of Normandy. Nevertheless, although Erwin had instantly recognised the senior officer in the room as 'the Brigadier,' I had no reason to doubt that this was the man to whom he had often referred in our conversations and in his memoirs relating to his time in Ukraine.

Shortly after his arrival in Ukraine, Erwin had served the 'Brigadier' as his valet, Erwin had been introduced to the stores by the 'Brigadier,' and later in France using his acquaintance with the 'Brigadier' saved him from a court martial when accused by a captain of stealing a case of wine. Even though technically an *Obersturmbannführer* was not a brigadier this is how Erwin, without hesitation on seeing the photograph, described Peiper. If Peiper was not the one to whom Erwin referred in conversations and his memoirs from his time as a 'valet' in Ukraine, Sepp Dietrich remained another possibility, after all Erwin had described the officer he had served as 'Judge S.' Something was being lost in translation or memory, or through denial and repression of memory. So, who was the 'Brigadier'? Peiper, Dietrich, or someone else? Or was there more than one senior officer in the life of Erwin and they had somehow become conflated in his memory over the years?

Sometime after Erwin's death I revisited the collection of Erwin's photographs with an even keener eye. Two dark, grainy images which I had previously dismissed because they were somewhat unclear, caught my attention. Both taken from some distance, but one closer than the other. Three officers were chatting at a roadside; one can hardly be seen at all in the shadows. In the distance is a staff car. I looked closer and enlarged one of the images as best I could. I became interested in the officer in the centre of the photograph; his epaulettes displayed the rank of what may well be a general (Plate 15).

I researched images of senior Leibstandarte personnel and found what could be a match for the officer in Erwin's photograph. The profile bore some resemblance to that of *SS-Oberführer* Kurt Meyer, *Oberführer* being a brigadier.

Meyer was a brutal leader responsible for significant war crimes on all the fronts the Leibstandarte served. In 1944, in preparation of the anticipated Allied landings in France, he was given charge of the newly formed 12th SS Panzer Division *Hitlerjugend*. For quite some time, the division managed to hold up the Canadian and British advance at Caen after D-Day, inflicting many losses but also conducting the Ardennes Abbey Massacre of Canadian PoWs. Meyer was captured just three days after Erwin in September 1944 when the headquarters were abandoned.

After the war it was reported by a former member of the SS that Meyer was responsible for one massacre that somehow resonates with one of Erwin's memories. A 25-year-old woman was shot while cooking lunch for a German and on the orders of Meyer all the inhabitants of the village were killed and their homes set on fire.[xix] Two surviving witnesses claimed the massacre took place on 17 February 1943, five days after the Leibstandarte had arrived in Semyonovka and Yefremovka.

In another incident, two SS officers had been wounded by retreating Soviet soldiers. In reprisal 872 men, women, and children were killed by the Leibstandarte. Approximately 240 were burned alive in a church. It was claimed that the battalion that carried out the massacre was led by Joachim Peiper.

Tragically this may have been an all-too-common incident. Whether this one was the one Erwin recalled will never be known. What cannot be denied is that Erwin was closely linked to Peiper at some point. While I am not wholly convinced the photograph is of Meyer, because the insignia may well be of an even higher rank than an *Oberführer*, it still places Erwin in the presence of very senior SS officers.

Chapter 18

CONFRONTATIONS AND DENIAL (2023)

On the last day of May 2023, I arrived at Erwin's bungalow, as I often had over the previous twenty years, expectant, hopeful, but realistically so, knowing from experience that the time together might bring fresh insights but, equally so, may not. I could not help but notice how overgrown the once manicured garden was, the paint was pealing in large patches from the garage door and the net curtains looked tired and greyish. I brushed past the untidy plants that bordered the path alongside the front window, rang the bell, and tried the door, understandably it was locked. I remembered the code to the key safe, Erwin's date of birth, and opened the door.

The home of an elderly person hit me as it had done on the last few occasions. Erwin was welcoming me from the lounge even before I could enter and see him. 'Allo … well, well, well!'

As I entered the lounge he was standing before me to the right of the dining table as he had so often done. His posture did not look as though it had worsened since my previous visit, he was somewhat shorter than once had been the case of course and slightly bent. Bright grey eyes raised to meet mine through the lenses of his glasses, the belt of his trousers so much higher in proportion to the rest of his body.

He was fascinated that I had been able to screenshot images from Google Earth of some of the places where his photographs had been taken including the shop where his film had been developed on Rue Porte-aux-Saints in Mantes.

He was quiet and reflective as we began looking at the images on my laptop. He smiled and chuckled at the photographs of him and his comrades relaxing in the sun. He did not recognise the pin ups on the wall behind him in what must be one of the earliest selfies. Much later

I did wonder if one of them was not Lillian Harvey, German actress, which is interesting because she fled the Nazi regime, first to France and then to the US.

Erwin instantly recalled the moment he was photographed wearing a heavy greatcoat. The faces of his colleagues were familiar, but he could not recall them. Sight of him in uniform initiated a recounting of his time in the Brussels cell and he informed me for the first time that he had also disposed of part of his unform, not least the 'Adolf Hitler' band on his left arm which indicated he was a member of the LSSAH. There was much silence on the part of Erwin, and expressions of 'dear, dear.' We came to a photograph of men standing at the back of a lorry loading or unloading something and I wondered if it was a dead animal; but Erwin was not so sure. He felt it could have been dead people, which he said he had seen a lot of. It was a shock, he said, to be there with a camera, and to take pictures takes a bit of thinking. 'First of all, the shock, when I saw I don't know how many people and we saw so many.' He then re-enacted with his arms swinging bodies onto a truck. I asked if he meant bodies taken back to barracks, no, 'it was at the Front.' Were they Germans, Russian PoWs, or civilians? He quickly replied that he did not see many civilians, only women because the men had already left. What is fascinating is his disclosure that his camera was always with him, that he was taking photographs of all manner of things, clearly those that could have informed us even more of his wartime service were no longer available to us. However, it is amazing what did survive as we shall see.

He chuckled and claimed to remember the photograph of him beside the Livarot town sign. He looked so young and he said it was 1942, just after the first Russian tour. He was 20. I asked him what he had already seen, he did not reply. I asked what it was like in France and he said he was constantly thinking of what may lie ahead, of how to avoid danger, always looking for a way out. One man in a group of three, including Erwin looking up at him in seeming admiration, brought about instant recognition. The Mantes Palais de Justice brought about a big smile. He acknowledged this was where he served the 'Judge,' saying that he was always busy, dealing with cases for the troops. A screenshot of the building today shocked him.

'The Judge had a very peculiar habit, shall we say, which surprised me, if you drive round, he would say let's go here or there. Then it is getting dark and they didn't like him, so they turned the lights out on him, but he always had a candle in his pocket.'

The photographs of what look like French women sitting in the back of a Kübelwagen led him to state that he was too innocent to realise when a woman was throwing herself at him. Looking at the photograph later, it looked as though one was picking at a bunch of grapes.

He instantly knew that one photograph of him was with a cat in his arms. I could not see it at the time and quickly passed over it; but sure enough, later I was to enlarge it and there was a kitten. Erwin had remembered the context sixty years after the photograph had been taken.

He recounted the villages burning and saw 'one of our boys setting fire to a roof and I couldn't understand.' He claimed not to have seen any killings in the villages.

One of the most detailed photographs was of the troop train passing through Cottbus station with branches from an oak tree stuck to the side of the wagon.

In his memoirs, Herbert Maeger recalled that a few hours after the journey had begun excitement grew amongst the men when it became apparent that they were heading West, and not the central front at Leningrad.[xx] He spoke of a summer sun and clear skies which tied in with Erwin's photograph of some men sunning themselves on the wagons.

We then came to the photograph of Peiper with others playing cards. During the online call Erwin had clearly stated the man smoking the cigar was 'the Brigadier.' Now, confronted with the image at the table in his living room Erwin claimed he did not know who he was. I informed him that it was Peiper, to which he then acknowledged he was. There were many sighs, Erwin's voice dropped whenever he broke the lengthy silences as he stared at the image on the laptop.

I asked if it was a shock and suggested that he did not consider that I would know who Peiper was. He nodded his head. 'Well, I saw him,' he said. Then more long pauses, it was clear Erwin was reluctant to continue with this thread. 'I didn't take much notice at the time.' Of what? Of the fact that Peiper was such a senior officer? Surely not? Of what was happening? Surely not? Was it just all in another day's work? Who can say?

I pointed out that Peiper was Himler's adjutant. There was much smacking of Erwin's lips, a deep sense of being elsewhere fell across Erwin's demeanour. I stated that Peiper had arrived in Ukraine in October 1941, just when Erwin arrived. I put to Erwin that he was with him. Peiper is seen smoking a cigar, which he said the Brigadier enjoyed. I asked if he knew what happened to him after the war. Erwin claimed he did not. So, I gave him an overview. I spoke of the trial at Dachau, of the crimes he was found guilty of, of his death sentence being commuted to life imprisonment, to that being reduced, of his release, of his attempts to work in Germany, of his return to France, of being recognised by French communists, of his death. 'Well, well, well,' – the classic response from Erwin. Then I was surprised to see Erwin smiling broadly. I asked him why. He said that this just showed that he did not have his camera ready on every occasion, that he had once had Erwin Rommel in his car and he did not take a photo of him, which he clearly regretted. However, after Erwin's death, I was to locate a photograph of Rommel with Sepp Deitrich south of Caen on 28 June 1944, a time when Erwin, as we shall see later, may well have been Deitrich's driver.[xxi]

Erwin then acknowledged I had done a lot of work, and the old chess player was looking cornered but pleased about it.

Was it Peiper who had asked him to get a horse for him to ride? 'I think so, yes.' This admission was the catalyst for Erwin to launch into a short tirade at the fate of Hitler's private telephone operator, whom I subsequently came to know as Rochus Misch and who was somewhat more than a telephonist being Hitler's personal bodyguard and last person to see him alive. Erwin spoke of him being sent to Russia and said something rather curious: 'the change in him – I could not believe it, you know.'

This raises a couple of questions: firstly, how had he seen him? On TV in a documentary? Possibly. Surely not in person. Or did he? However, his comment raises the second question: how did he know that Misch had changed? Since when? Reflecting on this now, and discovering from his 'niece' Martina that Erwin had informed her that he knew Misch, I suspect that Erwin had been in his company at some point; and if it was during the war then this would have put Erwin in close proximity to Hitler, perhaps when he drove a senior officer, Deitrich or Peiper, to meet with him, we will never know. This would also fit with Martina later telling me that Erwin had once revealed that he had visited the Wolf's Lair, Hitler's Eastern Front Headquarters, at some point. This admission came when he discovered that Martina's mother had been born nearby.

Without pausing he said, 'I hope when I can put something in writing, I can find the right words to make people understand what all this fighting was about.' He then lamented what was happening in Ukraine since the Russian invasion of 2022. It felt like a distraction, so I returned to the telephone operator as a lead back into his own service. Acknowledging that Misch could not have disobeyed Hitler, did he, Erwin, feel that he was in a similar position, unable to act in any other way? 'Yes, I didn't give any orders to go and shoot. These were ordinary people, you know.' The people who did the shooting?

Were they ever reluctant, the guys who did the shooting? 'Not that I know of, no. There were very few times when I was actually in the Front.'

The time for farewell had come. The two hours of intense conversation, prodding and hiding, being transported to another time and place, another world even, were over. Erwin was getting tired though he assured me he was fine. We shook hands once more as we always did on arrival and departure. His eyes pierced into mine. He had expressed surprise at how much I knew about the context of his past, he had done so before, but today it was as if I had pushed the door ajar, taken a peep inside, and spotted a few things that could lead on to another room.

However, I remember thinking, 'but not today, not today, or maybe ever. It may not be for me to know. Maybe these are the only clues I will ever have to form some kind of opinion on Erwin. Maybe this is all there is to know, and even if there were more, would a man who has deeply buried those clues for almost eighty years suddenly want to tell what remains in his memory of them? Even if he could, would he?'

At that moment I felt we had reached the limit of what Erwin was able or willing to disclose. As we bid farewell I could not help but wonder if we would ever see each other again. The thought had crossed my mind at the end of previous visits. But things could not go on as they were doing for ever. He seemed to defy the years, for sure they were taking their toll, but who else was left to tell of what he had witnessed?

Chapter 19

A RECKONING

For over twenty years I wrestled with what this relationship was about. Accepting Erwin's invitation to meet with him in early 2004 was my natural and pastoral response as a Christian minister to any encounter with a stranger. However, I must admit that the context, a Holocaust Memorial event, and the conversation we had, created within me a sense of intrigue. Over time that sense of intrigue deepened, sometimes diminished, for a while vanished altogether, and then it rose again. The unusual encounter, unusual for me at least, with a German veteran of the Second World War, stirred something within me.

Before meeting Erwin I had met with many British veterans and several Holocaust survivors. To have the opportunity to converse with a German veteran who might offer an additional perspective to those that I had gleaned previously was attractive. However, the fact that I counted several Holocaust survivors as friends meant that I was also somewhat uncomfortable about sitting with a German veteran whose service was initially unknown to me. Later, on occasion, I was to become more than a little anxious at my early suspicions that Erwin may have been a member of the SS. Erwin's early visible and vocal claim of 'not knowing anything about it,' which I took to mean the death camps, offered some reassurance as he was so convincing. To this day, in the absence of clear evidence, I cannot say for sure whether he knew of the death camps or not. However, from reading Volume 1 of his memoirs, there is no doubt that he knew of concentration camps because of the temporary incarceration of a neighbourhood friend in Berlin. This was clearly an awful experience for Erwin's friend:

> At 15 to 16 years old, we had formed a group of friends and met regularly and did what boys do. One day one of the gang was missing. Nobody knew what had happened to him. Some time had passed before he was

> back in the gang. Naturally we asked him 'Where have you been?' When he told us that he was in a concentration camp, we were shocked. 'What was it like?' we wanted to know. 'If I talk about it, I will be back in tomorrow' was his answer.

To be completely honest, there were occasions when a part of me did not want to know all the details of Erwin's service; satisfying one's intrigue is one thing, actively pursuing an investigation another. This was a significant matter for me, as I firmly believed Erwin considered me as his minister, his chaplain, his padre, his confessor. What he chose to share with me was up to him. I felt that pressing him to tell me more would have been wrong of me in my position and perhaps inappropriate for the relationship that had formed. Given time and trust, he slowly revealed more. This was so without me being too challenging with him.

This was clearly evidenced by the fact that the conversations lasted over so many years without much detail of his service. Then the relationship paused for quite some time after I moved from Taunton and took up residence in Lincoln. In one sense the relationship that we had experienced up till then probably ceased to be. For me my entire view of it shifted the day I did the internet search and confirmed that Erwin had been a member of the Waffen SS and that I could now identify him as a member of the SS Leibstandarte Adolf Hitler.

After a little further research, I learnt of the history and actions of the Leibstandarte. I then felt a sense of horror that the man I knew so well had been a member of a unit that was one of the worst in the Nazi regime. All sorts of emotions rose within me. Should I have been more brazen in my questioning early on? Should I have not been so gentle with him? Should I have abandoned the pastoral role and taken on the role of a historical researcher? Should I have told others of my earlier suspicions? Would that have betrayed Erwin? Had my silence and this relationship already betrayed victims of the Holocaust? Had my actions, or inaction, resulted in justice not being done? Should Erwin have been investigated by others?

Then there was the knowledge that thousands upon thousands of people had been members of the Waffen SS. No less than 900,000 including non-Germans. They surely could not have all been war criminals; could they? Were the lower ranks responsible? Camp guards, and clerks in the Death Camps were still being brought to trial shortly before I discovered that Erwin was a member of the SS. Their presence in the camps at certain times could be verified. They went about their duties knowing that tens of thousands would die that day and that they would be part of the process. They were clearly guilty of being part of a joint criminal exercise. However, frontline troops were less likely to be prosecuted because their presence at an atrocity could not always be verified due to a lack of documentation. Unless, of course, as in the case of atrocities such as the Malmedy massacre, where the killers could be identified and faced justice.

At Malmedy more than eighty US PoWs were gunned down by members of the Leibstandarte. One of my first explorations after discovering that Erwin was a member of this very same unit was to check the date of Malmedy. It turned out to be 17 December 1944. Erwin had been captured in Brussels over three months earlier.

When Erwin gave me permission in May 2021 to contact the *Bundesarchiv* to request any documentation they had of him, one of the records I received was akin to a personnel card which appeared to show that on 15 March 1965 the authorities had indeed checked Erwin's whereabouts reporting him to be 'wounded' on 2 September 1944. This understandably reassured me, though I had also come to learn of numerous other atrocities attributed to the Leibstandarte during the time of Erwin's active service, many on the Eastern Front from October 1941 through to the summer of 1943, and a number in Italy in October 1943. The record provided by the *Bundesarchiv* indicated that Erwin was admitted to an SS Korps Field Hospital in Charkow (Kharkiv) with gastritis or dysentery 29 May 1943 at a time when the battle for Charkow was waging and many atrocities were carried out by the Leibstandarte. Again, the record indicated that Erwin was admitted to another SS Korps Field Hospital at Castelnovo di Sotto Parma on 3 October 1944, two weeks after the infamous Boves massacre (300km away) and a week and a half after the massacre at Lake Maggiore (more than 200 km away). None of the records could locate Erwin at the scene of the crimes.

In 2018, twelve months before discovering Erwin's unit, my book *Echoes of Contempt* had been published. This addressed the terrible history of religious, and later racial and political, hostility of Christian Churches towards Judaism and Jews. In it, I sought to express with candour my own complicity prior to learning something of this tragic history and admit that there was still so much more to learn and do. Thankfully, I had shredded my old sermons many years before and I could not go back to them and witness the naiveté and likely unintended prejudice of my theology. When I read about the appalling behaviour of the Methodist Church leadership in Germany in the 1930s, I am a British Methodist, I wondered where I would have stood had I been born in Germany at the turn of the twentieth century.

Embarrassingly, and with a great deal of shame, my research had led me to believe that as a German Methodist I would have likely been at least a bystander, if not firmly supportive of the Nazi regime. Otto Melle, leader of the German Methodists, was so enamoured of Adolf Hitler that he described him as divinely appointed, that in his view there was a divine purpose to what was taking place in Germany, and that Melle wished this had happened earlier.[xxii] It is an uncomfortable truth that millions of good people subscribed to these views. Even those that did not support the Nazis were prepared to fight to the death in order not to lose a second war. This determination had grown partly because of the devastating economic impact of defeat in 1918. In Amy Buller's remarkable collection of essays, *Darkness Over Germany,* detailing conversations she held with Germans in the 1930s, this resolve came out on several occasions, even amongst those who were not supportive of the Nazi regime:

> 'But I shall fight – we all, although outside the Party, will fight to the last drop of our blood to see that we get the chance to make the Peace Treaty and not France or England (sic).' A German officer after Munich.[xxiii]

Of course, fighting a war in defence of your homeland is one thing, committing atrocities is another thing entirely. It was this possible aspect of Erwin's circumspection over the years that gave me the greatest concern, even though I had become fully aware of the likelihood that, given the same circumstances, I and many of my colleagues and friends could have fallen in line with the regime that slaughtered so many.

In the summer of 2023, just over three years after I first became aware of Erwin's membership of the Waffen SS, I took the opportunity to meet with a consultant psychiatrist who had a special interest in forensic psychiatry to discuss the relationship Erwin and I had. The psychiatrist worked in a top security hospital for those deemed to pose a danger to themselves or others. Therefore, he was hugely experienced in dealing with severe trauma and the psyche of those convicted of very serious crimes. It was a truly helpful encounter.

I had already considered some of the issues we addressed. In some instances, it was good to have some of my understanding affirmed despite my somewhat amateurish analysis in comparison. However, there were also new insights that helped me enormously to consider for the first time other underlying issues that may have been present in the twenty-year-long relationship with Erwin.

Erwin, like millions before him and since, wherever in the world, was conditioned by military service. He was taught to obey orders without flinching, let alone thinking, and evaluating. As someone growing up when and where he did, and as a member of the Hitler Youth, Erwin was exposed to an ideology we now rightly recognise as abhorrent. However, place, circumstance, the evolution of political thought, and propaganda, made that ideology a truth for those predisposed to it.

As a member of the Waffen SS, Erwin underwent further brainwashing. He will have become dehumanised by the combination of military training and Nazi ideology. In such a worldview, non-Aryans and enemies of Nazism were a threat to the glorious future of Germany. Those 'enemies,' including and especially the Jews, were deemed responsible for the decline of Germany over centuries. Recapturing an imagined past was the ultimate aim of the Nazis and the SS. Killing those that stood in the way of this goal was seen to be doing a great service for the Fatherland. The usual military objective of believing that the enemy had to be eliminated at all costs to protect family was added to by the craving to build the Thousand Year Reich. Of course, the actions of the SS went far beyond the normally accepted methods of defending a homeland, but because they were seeking to create a completely new civilisation, extermination became conventional.

Erwin and his comrades may not have fully appreciated their direct role in this or probably would not admit to it even if they were, but this is the way he and millions were led. The dehumanising of the enemy is a common feature of training a soldier to kill. If the person opposing you is no longer human, then pulling the trigger or using a blowtorch on a thatched building occupied by Slavs, becomes that less troubling. The soldier no longer has feelings for people on the other end of their actions. It is driven into them that this is merely a job, and a truly worthwhile, even honourable one at that. There is no need for the perpetrator to sense shame or guilt at the time, otherwise their effectiveness on behalf of the regime is lessened or lost even. What would have been wholly unacceptable and completely unthinkable to the individual in peace or more normal times, becomes the norm in war.

Over time, should the soldier survive the war, they may become aware of the impact of their actions, bringing them great trauma. In Erwin's case there was understandably a lot of stigmas attached to his allegiance. Not only was he a German military veteran living in the UK and the USA, but he was a member of the Waffen SS. In many cases German veterans resident in the UK after the war often became accepted and assimilated. Their new neighbours saw them as humans after all, which to a degree may seem surprising owing to the accounts of British veterans, newsreels and of course the bombing the British had experienced. However, the SS remained the truly dark side of the Nazi war machine, understandably so. They were seen as loyal to and vile instruments of Hitler's pursuit for global domination, while Wehrmacht veterans even came to be seen as 'victims' of the regime's propaganda. Whether such a claim about the Wehrmacht is wholly accurate or not is debatable.

When I began to analyse more dispassionately the relationship we had, and with the help of the consultant psychiatrist I began to understand a little more of Erwin's psyche, although no definitive conclusions could ever be drawn. Erwin was clearly a damaged person. He may have exuded an air of confidence, but he was a damaged man, nonetheless. There were his repeated references to the way his father hid from him the fact that his birth mother had died. He remained angry at his father for sending his sister to work in domestic service without him knowing in advance and therefore unable to bid her goodbye. He was hurt by the fact that his father never told him where she was and he had no idea at the time what had happened to her. The claim that his stepmother had sexually abused him weighed heavily on his mind.

Constantly referring to these incidents pointed to a man still struggling with his early years. The context of his teenage years also played a massive part in creating the man that he became, how could it not? He would have had few choices in his life.

On a couple of occasions after our relationship was renewed in 2020, I asked about his memories of Kristallnacht, the 1938 pogrom that claimed many Jewish lives and destroyed businesses and synagogues. On the first occasion he went silent, shook his head, and claimed he could not remember. I left it for a long time before I asked again. On the second occasion he took a deep breath and said he could not understand why this was happening. His friend threw a brick through a shop window and Erwin said he asked him why he had done this. Whether Erwin felt shame or guilt at the time is not possible to say, though he did appear to be displaying regret when he recounted this episode to me more than eighty years later. How much was this regret present in the early post-war years? Was it in evidence at all? We shall never know. Erwin's recollections can only ever be heard through the lens of time and the accumulated reflection that may or may not have taken place over those decades.

If Erwin was not directly involved in the shooting of Soviet prisoners or civilians, including Jews, he would have had no choice about being a witness to such crimes, even if it could be proven that he was present at the time. Nor could he have done much had he have heard accounts of atrocities from his comrades. I do believe him when he said that he did not know about the death camps, but I cannot help but feel that he was too close to the events for him not to know about what has become known as the 'Holocaust by Bullets', the systematic killing of Jews in Nazi occupied territories in the east.

The problem for Erwin, and so many like him, was that he had been conditioned to accept this as the norm, indeed that it was for the greater good. This is evidenced by the number of photographs taken by witnesses and perpetrators at the sites of atrocities, even sent home as a record of what was happening. It was all so normalised because the victims were not just enemies of the Third Reich, they were dehumanised, and in the Nazi mind-set, the world had to be rid of them. It was only much later that Erwin would have begun to rewire his moral compass and revisit the events in his memory with a different perspective. He would ask himself, as he informed me, why thatched roofs were being torched in Ukraine. As we have seen, the women offering hospitality to those that had come to kill them was a particularly troubling memory for Erwin. I cannot help but feel that this sense of regret may have been the later Erwin reflecting on the incident, not the Erwin of the time. The hospitality had contradicted what he had been taught and believed about the enemy; their generosity in the face of threat, and probably great fear, had taught Erwin they were human after all. When those feelings began to rise within him is anyone's guess. The frequent recounting of this event and others in the final years of Erwin's life could indicate that it may have been some time after the war that the process began.

Yet so much of the old Erwin remained, not least the jollity with which he greeted the photograph of his comrades sunning themselves on top of a troop train then laughing about the fact that they forgot to duck when they went under a bridge and were killed; additionally, the admission that he knew how to stack bodies in a truck in such a way as to get the most out of the space. Recounting these memories exposed me to the younger man, the soldier accustomed to death, the one who had built around himself a shield to deflect the shock and horror. Of course, each time Erwin recounted one of these incidents be they either hints of regret or a display of the young, cold, cynical, SS Erwin, still present in the likable, jovial old neighbour, it could have been Erwin subconsciously testing my own reactions, to gauge my own view on that which he was sharing. Naturally, I would be at one with him on the regret about the torching of Ukrainian dwellings and hospitality. However, how would I react to the packing of bodies and the casual deaths of sunbathing comrades? Was he, even if he did not know it himself, testing out the waters to see how I would respond?

I came to believe that the consequences of sharing his entire experience would have been too great for Erwin. His defence mechanism normalised the events to protect him from the reality of the horror, and revisiting them too often, and in too much detail, would probably have destabilised the older Erwin whose moral compass had surely shifted with the decades. The talks he gave to Church and Men's Groups later in his life, on his days as a PoW, never of his time in the military prior to arrest, were attempts to begin touching the waters of the past and checking to see how far the ripples went. They were probably the means by which he could at least begin the process of unburdening himself.

What I think he gained from telling me something of his experiences that were not included in the talks was the gradual addressing of those things that were deeply troubling him. He had not been able to address them properly in the post-war years, he could not meet up with old comrades, not that I know of, and everything had to be held close lest his new work colleagues, neighbours, and church members discover his past identity.

The measured nature of his disclosures may not only have been for Erwin's benefit. Whether he was able to recognise it in his mind or not, he may also have been seeking to protect me in some way, as his listener and maybe confessor. What if he had been completely candid with me? Was it not safer to test out the waters and gauge my reaction not only for his benefit but also for mine? Revealing too much too soon might have destabilised our relationship as well as exposed each of us to scrutiny. Neither were ready for full disclosure, for Erwin there needed to be someone with whom he could safely share his experience and over time I became that person.

That is not to say that I have now become his apologist, far from it. It is not my place, nor would I want it to be my place, to justify in any way his membership of the Leibstandarte let alone anything he may have done during his war years. He knew this, I told him so on more than one occasion. My interest was not in exonerating him or the actions of his unit. It was the case, and it remains the case, that forgiveness for these things is not in my gift. However, thanks to the length of time we knew each other and the non-judgmental manner I approached our conversations, except to a degree in those final days after discovering that he was Peiper's valet, Erwin came to trust me greatly. This was so even though I had remained sceptical at every stage as to what I was hearing was all that there was to know. The key to the watch Erwin held back from the young British soldier in that holding camp in France in the late summer of 1944 was never quite handed over to me. At no point did I think Erwin had shared all that he could have shared. I still believe there was more to know.

There were plenty of occasions when I wondered if I wanted to hear everything, and sometimes I concluded that I probably did not. He was 101 when he finally admitted to being Peiper's valet and driver. He was growing frail. His secrets had been kept for a long time and not all of them would ever be shared even if they could have been remembered at this stage.

I admit that I had been part of his relief. Some might ask whether he deserved to be relieved of his burden. To be honest I cannot say, nor can anyone else unless they know more about Erwin than I. He may be judged to be guilty by association, or worse, but so were hundreds of thousands of others and they went free, whether they told their stories or not.

It is right that those who gave the orders, those that pulled the triggers, and those directly responsible were brought to justice. It was right that Nazi war criminals were hunted down to their dying days. It is right that the perpetrators of any crime, including crimes conducted during war, face judgment. However, what is not correct is for any of us to be so self-righteous that we pass judgement on someone without the evidence required to be without any reasonable doubt. In Erwin's case there appears to be no evidence whatsoever of direct involvement in any atrocity. So far as I can tell, there is nothing to confirm him as complicit in any decisions that took the lives of the innocents, let alone evidence to suggest that he himself may have been part of a round up or massacre. As a driver it may well have been the case that Erwin drove the commander to or from an atrocity, in which case he would be guilty of joint criminal enterprise, the get-away driver so to speak. However, I do not believe this can be proven. Without the photograph, without any document, without any eyewitness, or without a formal admission, Erwin is surely akin to those hundreds of thousands of Waffen SS who could have never faced trial.

Chapter 20

NEARING THE END GAME (JANUARY 2024)

He still managed to fill the room even though he had become physically diminutive since we met previously. The chair on which he had sat for so long had now become a part of him, no longer a structure on which to temporarily support his great strength but a buffering cushion that was his only bodily protection. His neck no longer seemed to exist. It had disappeared somewhere into his chest, and his head was perched on his once proud but now rounded shoulders. The clothes he wore had become too large for him, the belt of his trousers further up his torso. Dry crumbs were scattered across his woollen waistcoat. Notwithstanding this unavoidable decline for someone approaching his 102nd birthday the recognisable sound of joy issued from him on hearing my greeting. The old grey eyes were still razor sharp, crisply focussed on my own. His smile, which I had become so acquainted with over the twenty years of our conversations, swept across his face. The radiance, so familiar to all those who met Erwin, cast light across the increasingly cluttered room. His hand reached out to mine. It was clear that he had retained the ability to command attention.

I had received news from Rebecca that Erwin wanted to see me, that he was feeling unwell and that he had no idea how long he had left in this world. On arriving at the bungalow, I was concerned to find two cars at the property. I was relieved to see Erwin in his chair. One car belonged to a carer and another to two of his friends from the neighbourhood who kept an eye on him. The carer was about to leave, and it seemed that the two friends had waited for me to exchange contact details and to ensure that I would be able to fulfil Erwin's request to conduct the funeral once the inevitable happened. Once they had left Erwin cut to the chase.

Gone was the playful Erwin who had enjoyed teasing me with a titbit about the war, then engaging in distraction the moment I showed any enthusiasm to dig deeper. It was as if there was not to be another opportunity; this was it. He grinned widely as if the battle was over and he had been cornered. He then said he had been taken by complete surprise the moment I had confronted him with the documentation proving him to be a member of the Leibstandarte. His hands were not held up in surrender, but he knew he had fought well, keeping the secret hidden from others for eighty years and from me seventeen. If frustrated at times I had always felt up to the task, time, after all, had in all probability been on my side, the question was always if time was on Erwin's side. It had been a case of simply being there, of allowing him to develop his trust in me if he so wished. There had been a sense of not having much choice. Erwin had seen something in me that led him to think that I could have been the one to share his story and pass it on. He said as much.

I understood from my first visit to his and Anne's home that in order to allow him to tell his story, it had also been necessary to permit him to play his game, the one that had teased sergeants in the Leibstandarte barracks at Lichterfelde during initial training, that had enabled him to survive two tours of the eastern front and the invasion of Normandy, especially Caen. The same game that had conned a young Tommy into providing biscuits when in captivity. Undoubtedly the game for Erwin was now reaching its unavoidable conclusion, and he knew it. There were no more cards to play, there was no point in extending the game further. Erwin evidently wanted to draw on his memory one last time leaving nothing more for him to barter.

We did a little recap of the twenty years we had known each other. This reminiscence brought many smiles and not a little laughter. He even acknowledged how he had enjoyed the teasing, the dripping out of information, a trickle at first then in the last three years a growing surge. He said that I had surprised him with my ability and patience to retrieve his story – more importantly that I had worked out so much detail for myself from the morsels of information that had been part of his recollection. The fact that I had pieced together his years in the SS, the people he had worked with, and the events that he would have witnessed led him to deeply respect me.

Erwin raised with me that first encounter at the Holocaust Memorial Day event twenty years before. His joy in recollecting the occasion was in full evidence. Why had he gone, I asked him? Because he thought he might learn more, he responded. Why had he invited me for a coffee and a chat, I asked. Because he felt I might be someone he could trust, someone who would understand. He then grew more serious.

Our friendship meant a lot to him. I was moved.

He wanted to make sure I recalled the story from before the war of the person from his neighbourhood who was sent to a concentration camp, was released, and refused to talk about it for fear of being rearrested. He was proud of his father refusing to join the Nazi Party when approached at work, and that his father had quoted a text from the Bible in response. However, when Erwin pointed out that he needed to be in the Hitler Youth to become an apprentice engineer, his father had accepted it. Erwin maintained that he had never put on his Hitler Youth uniform. He confessed that he was admitted to the Leibstandarte on the grounds of his physique. That he had once been approached by an ex-girlfriend to be part of the Lebensborn programme and that he had refused. He was sad that he had never been able to discuss these things with his father even though his father was a veteran of the First World War.

After recalling some of the events to which he had referred on previous occasions, Erwin spoke at greater length than before on Sepp Dietrich. Previously he had claimed he could only recall seeing him come out of the latrine pulling his trousers up late one night whilst Erwin was on guard duty. But now he told me of the many times Dietrich had spoken to him when he was his driver; that Deitrich was 'an ordinary person, despite such a high rank.' Erwin spoke of facilitating the washing of Peiper's clothes, of getting him drinks and cigars. When I asked about what he thought of Peiper after the war and all the crimes had become evident Erwin acknowledged that he would have liked to have met him again and talked about old times, but that was not possible.

Then out of nowhere Erwin said he himself was 'not educated enough, too stupid' to have handled the situations. Asked again about Peiper's crimes and the trials, Erwin responded that despite his interest he only got snippets of information and was keen to share his concern that they were only being tried for what he believed the Allies themselves had done, an argument put by the defendants at the time. He was sad about the killings and concerned about what had happened to Soviet PoWs including a group of them that had surrendered to him. He claimed to have been confused as to why those in authority were not preventing the mass killing of people.

Even now at the age I am, I can only wrestle with how I might have acted in the circumstances Erwin found himself in; but at the time of these atrocities, he was less than a third my age. How possible is it to pass moral judgement on someone from a position of hindsight, with more significant knowledge, and the benefit of accumulated wisdom of the decades? Wrong was wrong, unequivocally so yes, but how capable was Erwin to make a rational and moral decision at his age, in the maelstrom of such political turmoil and the brutality of war?

Chapter 21

HIS EYES CLOSED FOR THE LAST TIME

It is 18 June 2025. Erwin has died. He was 103 years 2 months and 16 days old. It is twenty-one years and five months since we first met. How could either of us have known in January 2004, when he invited me to his home, how long that chat would take us? It seems strange now that there will not be any more chats, no more secrets to be disclosed, never again will I hear his familiar accented voice saying 'well, well, well.' Erwin was a presence in my life for more than two decades, a constant dilemma, at times a source of bafflement, and a curious 'privilege' to know, certainly a responsibility.

We had a pact. I would write his story and make it public after he had closed his eyes for the last time, as he so poetically put it. He was keen for people to know that story, and yet he was not at liberty to tell it himself. He clearly appreciated that someone had come into his orbit prepared to listen and learn, who already had a keen interest in the era. Yet he did not wish to be around to see the reaction of others when what he had witnessed, or been part of, became known, even though he never voiced it in this way. On a handful of occasions, he had told me that only I ever knew the 'full' story. I believe others must surely have heard fragments of it, and maybe some were able to fit the pieces together, even leading them to conclude that he was a former member of the Waffen SS. However, such was his skill at stringing people along when they wanted to get something from him, and his extraordinary ability to retain for himself what he thought of as important, the full story cannot be known even to me.

I guess I will never know for sure. I cannot overlook the fact that there are gaps in the story, especially his time in Italy. I do not think we can put this down to failing memory. It is quite possible he chose to recall the Russia and Normandy campaigns but pushed to the back of his mind, perhaps long before I met him, the few months he spent in Italy when Mussolini's regime fell. The actions of the Leibstandarte were certainly brutal at that time. If he did witness any of this brutality, he never disclosed it to me.

There are some aspects of Erwin that remain an enigma. There was something paradoxical about him. He was the avuncular neighbour, yet had his story become known impressions of him may have been different. He was both a troubled and playful man. He enjoyed interaction and controlling the conversation. He brought to bear what he had learnt from playing chess.

There is a real sense in which the incident in the holding camp in Northern France in the late summer of 1944 when as a PoW he withheld from the British guard the key to the pocket watch he had traded earlier for corned beef never left him, the strategy was played out time and again over the decades. It certainly was played out with me and I am sure it would have been so for others. But now Erwin has played his last game, and it hardly seems possible. We sometimes considered what would happen if he outlived me. We decided if that were the case one of my sons should take my place. The documents, photos, and memoirs Erwin had given me, alongside the notes I had taken, would be passed on to my son and published after Erwin 'closed [his] eyes for the final time'. There were a small number of occasions when I believed that this alternative plan might have to be put into action. However, that was not to be the case, and I even began to wonder if Erwin's determination to keep his story secret strengthened his will to survive. In the end, even he had to close his eyes for the last time.

So now the time has come to proceed with Erwin's wishes and seek to make his story known. I have no idea how others will react. I just know I committed myself to this a very long time ago and must see it through for all the reasons I have given, including that we should all continue to learn of the complexity of life, with all the dilemmas we face, the choices we make, and the mistakes that often ensue. The biggest lesson I learnt over the last twenty-one years is that it is impossible for me to say that I would have behaved in a clear and certain manner given the time and context of Erwin's teenage years. It is a lesson we would all do well to heed, for we might then assess more fully the choices that are before us and consider the consequences of the decisions we are about to make today and into the future. I am confident Erwin shared this belief too, which is part of the reason he wanted his story to be told. It is just that he knew the attention on him would focus instead on other aspects of his war years had it become known during his lifetime. This was an attention he did not want to experience; whether more would have been exposed as a result I cannot say.

This chapter was written immediately after I received the news that Erwin had died.

Chapter 22

A MEMORY AND A FAREWELL

There are many things that can trigger a memory, or a long-forgotten emotion, one that may have been suppressed or just lost in the passage of time: rediscovering a photograph that has not been seen for many years, of an event, of an old friend, or of a place; hearing a name from the past or a song that once stirred the heart. The digitised photographs certainly did that for Erwin. They sometimes raised a smile on his face as he recalled a building, a comrade, or even an event. Then there was his harmonica.

When Erwin learnt to play the harmonica I cannot say, I should have asked. However, what became apparent was that Erwin found it to be a useful instrument in transporting him from his room to another place altogether. I first became aware of this when Rebecca filmed our conversation on 10 August 2022.

Historian Rebecca had been a researcher and producer of well-known ancestry TV programmes tracing the family line of famous celebrities. During lockdown I approached her as a friend of my daughter-in-law in strictest confidence to conduct a little research into Erwin. This helped fill in a few but not many gaps. By the summer of 2022, I had introduced Erwin to Rebecca, and he was pleased that someone of such standing and experience was interested in his story. This had initially bothered me because I did not know how he would react, but he was both charmed by Rebecca and convinced his story would remain hidden until after his death. When we then put to him the possibility of Rebecca recording him giving an account of his wartime experiences with the intention of using it in a documentary in due course he was delighted. By now we had grown increasingly convinced that Erwin, at the age of 100, was almost certainly one of the last surviving veterans of the SS, especially of the SSLAH who served in Ukraine and Russia in the autumn of 1941.

When I arrived at Erwin's home on 9 August 2022, a bright Tuesday morning, Erwin was comfortable in his chair and looking very pleased with himself. Rebecca and her cameraman were already present when I arrived. Erwin and I were to be filmed in conversation with one another. It was difficult to replicate the informality and intimacy Erwin and I had forged over eighteen years of conversations, but by the end of the filming I believe there was enough footage to usefully slot into any future documentary. Erwin knew this would not be aired until after he had died. He knew that this was a significant moment, he seemed relieved that he had got things off his chest that otherwise he would have taken with him to the grave. Then I spotted the harmonica on the table. Out of nowhere, without any prior thought given to this, I asked if he had ever played *Lili Marlene*, the wartime classic for both sides, Marlene Dietrich's version for the Allies and Lala Andersen's for the Germans.

He then proceeded to pick his harmonica up and held it for a little while in deep thought. I knew that Rebecca's cameraman had put his camera away and something told me to pick my phone up and begin filming.

Erwin began to play. It was for me one of those moments when a chill runs down my spine and I guess I stopped breathing. He appeared to stare at me throughout the piece, but for much of the time I think he was elsewhere. We know that our own past, however long ago, can seem to have been very recent, even as if it were yesterday if our memory and emotions permit it to be so. I think for a moment Erwin was in a special place for him. As his rendition was ending his face was conveying a deep joy and then his eyes began to focus on mine. As he took the harmonica from his lips the smile swept across his face. I could tell that it wasn't just that he had done a good job, not just that he had pleased me by fulfilling my request and mirroring my own feelings at that time, but he had somehow revisited his past in a very real way.

Regrettably I pressed the stop button on my phone and ended the filming prematurely, only capturing the very beginning of the smile that Erwin went on to fully emit. I think I stopped recording because subconsciously I believed I could only breathe when he had stopped playing. The three of us burst into applause. The room had been filled with the sound of a bygone era.

Two years later, on one of my final visits, Erwin played harmonica again for me. This time hymns that meant a great deal to him, especially *Great is thy faithfulness*, and *How great thou art* before launching into *Lili Marlene*. The two years since he first played it for me had taken their toll on him, his breathing less secure, and his eyes glazed not just in age, but I believe in contemplation. He knew his time was short. He had known that for many years but there was no longer any doubt. He was 102 and his frailties were overtaking his strength and resilience, he was noticeably gaunter, his waist band higher up his stomach.

I decided to look up Lala Andersen's recording of *Lili Marlene* on a streaming service on my mobile phone. When it began to play, Erwin straightened himself as best he could, fixed his face into a look of resolve, and when Andersen began to sing, so did he, clear and strong, the German lyrics filling the room. Then, after a couple of verses Erwin put his harmonica to his lips and accompanied Andersen before singing again the closing verses. Sadly, it was unrecorded on this occasion because my phone was already in use, but it was a moment I shall never forget.

It was inevitable that we should choose Andersen's recording to enter the crematorium for Erwin's funeral on the afternoon of Friday 18 July. We also sang *How great thou art*, one of the Erwin's two favourite hymns. We ended with a recording of Erwin playing *Amazing Grace* on his harmonica. It was a fitting end to Erwin's life. His long-term friends Judith and Andrew, oversaw the arrangements. Erwin could not have remained in his home so long as he had, to the very end in fact, without their extraordinary care.

Many neighbours and friends from the area gathered to pay their respects. We acknowledged something of his past without details, as Erwin had requested. I have no doubt in my mind that what was not said was probably as significant as what was. The attendees seemed to appreciate that Erwin had a story which he had withheld from them to the last. However, it became clear that he had told many that he had entrusted me with it. Several people afterwards asked when the book would be published because they were keen to read it. I could not help but feel that this was classic Erwin – dangling a thread for interest to be piqued but leaving them hanging on for me to produce the closing chapters of their own relationships with him. It had fallen to me to hand over the rest. I can imagine Erwin displaying one of his sardonically rueful smiles, though gently and playfully so, at this.

It was at the funeral that Martina and I came face to face at last. Martina had been described by Erwin as his 'niece' although she was the daughter of a friend he had made while living in Hove some years before.

For some reason, Erwin had prevented me from contacting Martina during his lifetime, firstly telling me that she did not speak good English, which turned out to be false, and then giving me an incorrect email address for her but never getting round to giving me the correct one. Again, classic Erwin. As I mentioned before it became obvious to me that Erwin did not want us to share our stories of him, or, perhaps more importantly, the stories he had told each of us and comparing or confirming them.

We both delivered eulogies at the funeral. Although we had spoken a couple of times on the phone and via text after Erwin's death and before the day itself, we had not considered what each of us would say. As it happened, my view is that any member of the congregation would have thought we had. We both knew Erwin so well that our reflections complemented one another. Having led funerals for over forty years I knew this to be one of those that demanded much of me, yet it came together in tribute, sorrow, and not a little regret. To use the fashionable term, there was closure.

However, not many in our world, not perhaps in the congregation even, would know how much of a closure this funeral was. How could Erwin not be one of the last surviving members of the SS? Especially the Leibstandarte. Yet there could be no publicity, no media attention, no statements to that effect. We had to hold on to Erwin's request until everything was ready. His story, in the wrong hands, could easily have been presented in a very different perspective to the reality. I was adamant that I should do my very best to ensure that the complexity came through, the moral dilemma, the damage, the fear, the remorse.

The most important thing for me was, and remains, ensuring we all learn from this experience, of how a seemingly ordinary neighbour, a man of charm and wit, could have been swept up in the maelstrom of the Nazi war machine during his teenage years and early adulthood, like so many, sadly.

We can push so much to the back of our minds. We can deny what we have done in the distant past. We can 'move on', we can 'start again', we can pretend that we are a different person now, which to some extent we are, but the truth is that it may only take seeing a rediscovered photograph, or hearing a long-forgotten song, to transport us to an event or an age that defined us at the time. The emotions then rise, they are revisited, years have turned into days and we like Erwin, realised that the past has never truly left us.

Chapter 23

THE REALITY SINKS IN

A friend, concerned about any backlash I might face when I informed him of publishing an account of this relationship asked: do you think you will be criticised? My answer was unequivocal: yes, almost certainly. But what was I to do? Allow the stories to remain hidden? Would an archaeologist rebury a find that might enhance the understanding of previous discoveries? Return it to the darkness from which it emerged? Consign it to the silence thereafter for someone else to only hear of its discovery on the grapevine and tell the story without the firsthand experience of the initial recovery? The archaeologist has already disturbed the ground in which it has resided these past years and returning it would mean the evidence has already been tampered with. No, having retrieved the story it became incumbent upon me to tell it as I received it, providing another perspective to the millions of testimonies recorded of those years. Only through hearing from those witnesses and actors on all sides can we have any hope of beginning the process of considering the age-old question of why – the question that had been powerfully posed on the posters of genocidal images and loudly asked by the chaplain of all those present at the school event Erwin and Anne attended in 2004. Even now we may not be much better equipped to provide the answer to that eternal question. But by spending the next twenty years listening to someone who was present at the time on the side of the perpetrator, and recording what I discovered as faithfully as I could, did I have any hope of attempting a contribution to a response and in so doing move the debate along a little further for others to continue the journey.

Shortly after Erwin's death, I suddenly became even more aware of the enormity of the situation. Newsreel footage from the war filled my mind's eye, the soundtrack from a documentary accompanied the images, my breathing seemed to have paused, my eyes widened, my teeth clenched. The twenty years that had passed quickly, the conversations and revelations thrown into the air like photographs from an album falling randomly to the floor, out of sequence and devoid of context. How had I found the strength and patience not to disclose what I had heard and learnt? There had been an initial sense of relief alongside the realisation of loss. Then it hit me out of nowhere. I remained convinced that the path we had chosen was correct, my vocation demanded discretion and I had little or no choice but to guard his confidence and memory. For sure I had often pushed Erwin without putting him under undue pressure. However, I had always been aware of his frailty, particularly so in recent years. When he resumed contact in 2020, he was a man in his 98th year grieving for his wife of twenty-six years and whom he had adored for much longer. Over the final years of his life his health slowly deteriorated, and he became frailer and more vulnerable with each visit, with each call. I sometimes worried that drawing on his memories of the war years could have exacerbated his condition and should he have been taken ill or even died following a conversation then I could have been culpable. But now things had changed. He was gone.

He died slowly over several days without a recent visit from me. I had looked in my diary and had pencilled in a visit on Thursday or Friday. He died on the Wednesday. We had said what may have been our final goodbye almost every time I visited since the summer of 2020. On each occasion the thought that it could have been our final farewell passed through my mind. I am convinced Erwin would have thought so too. He had seen enough death to make him realise that rising at another dawn could not be taken for granted. Regrettably I cannot recall the details of our last phone call a week or so before he died. All I can remember is that it was brief and his voice was weak.

Erwin's death meant that his 'niece' Martina and I finally met. We spoke on the phone before the funeral and shared in the tribute on the day. For me, it was yet another example of how Erwin had played me and protected his past. When I first became aware of Martina some years before, Erwin had said she was living in Germany, didn't speak good English so it was of not much use for me to contact her. However, he relented and gave me her 'email address' which proved to be inaccurate when my email bounced back. It transpired that Martina, though German, also lived in England, spoke perfect English and had become a kind of surrogate niece because Erwin and her mother had been great friends when he, Vi and Anne, resided in Hove. I smiled because I couldn't help but feel that had I been able to confront Erwin with this newfound knowledge, he too would have smiled, chuckled even.

Along with Erwin's briefcase containing many documents, Martina handed me a photo album of Erwin's that I never knew existed. It contained photos from before and after the war. There appears to be a very small number from his days in captivity. Also included in the album were images of his family and, most poignantly, one of Erwin in the Hitler Youth uniform he claimed he never wore. This drove home the fact that though he claimed only I knew the 'full story,' I did not, he had taken some of it to the grave.

After the funeral, I also became aware of a deeper resonance with Erwin. As I reflected on his life, and particularly his early years, it struck home that we had both lost a parent before we had been conscious of them, I seven months before my birth, Erwin shortly after his birth. Both of us grew up with a step-parent with whom we experienced a challenging relationship. I had little in common with my stepfather and he with a stepmother who overlooked him in favour of her own younger offspring, even though she was his mother's younger sister. All of this made each of us what we were. At the time it was an unrecognised resonance, an unconscious factor despite the fact, with hindsight, it somehow acted as an understanding that had been beyond explanation. This only served to further endorse for me the view I had formed over the years, that I could so easily have been the one who had sat before me holding back certain experiences and struggling to comprehend involvement in something beyond my control.

It had become increasingly clear to me over the years that people are not always what you want them to be or expect them to be. What we have read, learnt, been taught, or led to believe, may not be entirely accurate when we are faced with the reality. Even an SS veteran may not be so easy to condemn, let alone hate, many years after the event, and once we have spent a long time in their company getting to know them as they are, or as they have become; perhaps somewhat confused, ashamed, and filled with regret, yet charming, considerate, and caring. Similarly, a neighbour whom we find to be so likeable, so personable, so kindly, and avuncular, may not be so easy to love after their possible complicity in one of the greatest crimes in human history becomes known to us. Hate and love, two extremes that seem impossible to conjoin may be more closely linked than we first thought.

After more than twenty years of conversations, where we often jostled and bartered with one another in Erwin's attempts to drip feed me with the information he wanted me to hear on that particular day, and I wanting to tease more details out of him without pushing too hard and silencing him for ever, I think it best to leave the last word to Erwin – which I know he would have liked.

It was in 2024, during our last conversation on the war because I felt that in subsequent visits it was too much to ask of him anything more, for it was clear to me that he had said all he wanted to say. I put to him a question. Which seemed appropriate because this account of our relationship began with his question to me so long before: 'Could it have been avoided?'

So, I asked, 'Erwin, if Peiper were sitting in this room with us now, what would you say to him?

At which Erwin fell silent for a little while, to me the room seemingly disappearing around us. He looked up and I could see from his eyes that he was elsewhere. Then his voice, even quieter than usual, responded: 'I would ask him why we did what we did.'

POSTSCRIPT

It was typical of Erwin to let you think you'd heard all he had to share, that the story was complete, only for him to take you by surprise with a new snippet. On occasions that additional information turned out to be a significant revelation. The previous chapter was meant to be the final one. However, just before this book went to print a supplementary one had to be written. This only served to reinforce my question as to whether we will ever know all there is to know about Erwin's wartime service, almost certainly not.

On the day of Erwin's funeral, following the post-service reception, Andrew, who together with Judith had acted as Erwin's executor, handed over the case of documents Erwin had set aside for me. It was an old brown leather attaché case. It measured 450mm x 250mm x 100 mm deep. So many documents and papers had been crammed in that it sprung open when I moved the catches. The aroma of the years emerged from the case. There was too much for me to take in on first sight and I managed to close it with some effort. Martina stood next to me with two of Erwin's old photo albums, she kindly handed me the one that contained some images from the war years.

I couldn't wait to view what looked like a fascinating and perhaps informative collection of documents and photographs. Opening the attaché case on the train journey would have been impossible as I feared spilling its contents. But my inquisitiveness got the better of me and I pored over the photo album. Thankfully the train was quiet and no one was near enough to overlook what I was viewing. What they would have made of it had they have seen, one can only guess.

The brown leather album had a folding clasp on the right and brown twine on the left spine holding the pages together. It measured 270mm x 190mm. It had been given to Erwin in 1953 by his brother and sister-in-law. It was inscribed using a white crayon on the grey card front page: *Zum Andenken Weihnachten 1953 aus der Heimat, Berlin* (as a memento of Christmas from your homeland). On the left-hand side in the same crayon were hand-drawn candles and baubles on a spruce branch. It was surely a Christmas present. Erwin had clearly enjoyed filling it with what photographs he had in his possession. A few were from the negatives he had given me previously, including the one of him visiting his brother while on leave with his brother bandaged from an injury. (Plate 8)

What did intrigue me were two formal, head and shoulder photos of Erwin in Hitler Youth uniform, something he said he had never worn. They were likely taken soon after he joined on 10 March 1937 just before his fifteenth birthday. This brought out a shake of my head and the thought that had crossed my mind so often over the decades: 'typical Erwin.' It felt as I was experiencing one last knowing smirk from beyond the grave. Other photos from both before and shortly after the war were fascinating. One of him aged two or three standing on a stool with presumably his sister embracing and kissing him, innocent of the years that lay ahead. Of children on their first day at school holding the obligatory cone (*Zuckertüt* because they carried sweets to sweeten the child's first day from home, or now known as *Schultüte* and are more likely to carry Lego or Playmobil and others items). One photograph shows Erwin looking incredibly smart wearing a suit and holding what looks like a Fedora-type hat in his right hand in 1936, standing next to a plinth with a Bible placed on it. The inscription on the back, probably written by his father that said 'my dear Erwin on his confirmation'.

The post-war photos were equally fascinating. Two or three looked like they had been taken during his POW days on a work detail in a rural area. There were quite a number of his visits to East Berlin, including one outside the factory he worked in as an apprentice, and another of his family at his childhood home which had remarkably survived. Martina would tell me that when he visited again decades later, after the Berlin Wall came down, a neighbour came out of her apartment and asked if he was one of the Stahlberg boys; he and his brothers must have made a big impression as young men. A shiver went down my spine when I heard this story.

On my arrival at home, I took out the documents from the attaché case, but there were too many to consider after such a long and exhausting, if not emotional, day. It took me weeks and months to go through them properly. When I did so I discovered they were mainly references, the sale agreement of his home in Connecticut, and a list of the homes he had lived in over the decades since his discharge. There were also travel documents and passports including his US citizenship certificate and passport. There were marriage certificates, Erwin's birth certificate, a large number of documents relating to his apprenticeship, his qualifications, and so much more. However, what was particularly exciting for me was a copy of Erwin's letter dated 27.7.1990 thanking the *Bundesarchiv* in Aachen for a copy of his *Soldbuch* following his request to consider his pension claim. The letter read: *Für die Heute erhaltene Dienstszeitbescheinigung, Mit beiggelegten Kopien meines Soldbuches Nr. 1532, möchte ich mich hiermit bedanken.* (For the service time certificate received today, with the enclosed copies of my pay book No. 1532, I would like to thank you hereby.) This confirmed what Erwin had earlier claimed, and my heart quickened. When he told me of secreting it in a palliasse (straw-filled mattress) in a Brussels cell on the night of his capture to avoid his captors discovering his unit and history he thought it was gone for ever. Until that is, he was taken by complete surprise by the response from the *Bundesarchiv* confirming his military pension due to him based on his wartime service complete with the copy of the *Soldbuch*. However, it soon became clear to me as I went through the documents in his attaché case that the copy was not there. It was missing. A document that would really add to the story. I quickly researched what an SS *Soldbuch* would have recorded. I even purchased a blank facsimile which I translated into English. It was extraordinary. It contained a wealth of information. Personal information, transfers to different units, provision of equipment, hospital admissions, leave, awards and so much more. But I didn't have Erwin's copy. What had happened to something he had clearly valued and had been excited at receiving? I could only imagine that at some point over the years he had destroyed it because of the detail of information contained within it and he didn't want others to know. At least I knew that the original existed in the *Bundesarchiv*.

Thankfully, Erwin had signed *Bundesarchiv* forms in May 2021 declaring that he gave permission for me to access all documentation on him held by them. Because of this I was able to apply again to the *Bundesarchiv* requesting a copy or access to the *Soldbuch*. However, I couldn't help but wonder why I hadn't received a copy four years previously in 2021. Had it been lost or destroyed at some point during the intervening years? Surely not. Had it been misplaced? Knowing the *Bundesarchiv* is based on various sites around Berlin and indeed in a small number of cities across Germany I began my quest.

As I anticipated, it took a long time to receive a reply. The copy could not be located. Martina kindly took up the challenge forwarding the 1990 letter to them from Erwin thanking them for the copy. The pension office was contacted; they had no record. We were sent to various sites to request information on the *Soldbuch's* whereabouts. It took time. It was frustrating, increasingly so. Eventually I received several documents, some were duplicates of what I had received four years earlier. Nevertheless, others were included that were new to me. These were a copy of the card that reported Erwin missing and copies of two letters sent to Erwin's father informing him of this fact. The first was sent on 22 September 1944 just nineteen days after his capture which sketched out his last known whereabouts.

> SS Rottenführer Stahlberg was the driver of Haupsturmführer X (redacted to protect his descendants) and was present during the collection of motor vehicles from Brussels in the company of the same. Stahlberg was last seen in Brussels on 2.9.44. It is therefore assumed that Stahlberg also fell or was taken prisoner.

This confirmed Erwin's account without mentioning that the *Haupsturmführer* insisted on filling the *Kübelwagen* full of loot and bringing his mistress along!

A more sombre and comprehensive letter was sent to Erwin's father a month later on 23 October expressing sadness that no news had been received on his son. It was assumed that Erwin and the officer had been attacked or fallen into enemy hands. As we know from Erwin's testimony, only Erwin survived the attack, the officer and his mistress were killed instantly. It would not be until February or March 1946 that Erwin's father would receive news that his son had been captured a full eighteen months earlier. This is evidenced from the card retained by Erwin's father which was passed on to Erwin at a later stage. The standard card contains little information other than Erwin was a POW in Camp 102. The Camp is not named on the card but we know that this was Llanddarog, Carmarthenshire where he had been transferred on 10 January from Haverfordwest, Pembrokeshire.

Finally, after exercising much patience, I sent a fairly curt letter to the *Bundesarchiv.* I stated that I had been sent from one site to another and then to a third before being sent full circle back to the first site. On each occasion I had been told the *Soldbuch* was not at that site and I should try another. Just a fortnight later at the end of May 2026 I received a welcome reply. The *Soldbuch* had been located and scans of it were attached. At last. It felt as if I had arrived at the end of a Treasure hunt and the prize was ready to be unwrapped. However, I was on holiday when it came so I only had my phone to access it, the images were blurred and the text impossible to read. Thankfully we were with our family and my younger son had his laptop with him. Having transferred the attachment to his laptop meant that I could spend a very happy hour staring and trying to decipher some of the pages, though the handwriting was more often than not beyond me. Nonetheless, here was the document that Erwin had spoken of on numerous occasions, the one he had last held on the evening of 3 September 1944 in a Brussels cell awaiting interrogation and an uncertain future, the possibility of death hanging over him. I recall how shocked he had been when he recalled seeing the copy in 1990 which had been posted to him, that the bottom corner had been damaged after he had hidden it, 'I kept it with me in perfect condition throughout my service.' This damage to which Erwin referred was indeed immediately apparent to me. But so too was a strip of brown tape over the spine holding together the front and back pages. It was roughly cut and I suspect that this had been done after the 1990 copy had been sent to Erwin, otherwise I am confident he would have mentioned it.

His first formal photograph in his SS Leibstandarte Adolf Hitler uniform was double stamped on the inside front cover. I was keen to know if anything within the *Soldbuch* confirmed or brought into doubt anything Erwin had told me. There was nothing in the *Soldbuch* that would lead me to question anything of Erwin's accounts. If anything, the details added more to it. There were two in particular. Firstly, I recalled one of his photographs of a comrade standing outside a house, possibly in France as he was in a summer shirt. He was carrying a side arm (plate 16). When I showed this to Erwin, he commented that the man was clearly guarding someone of importance in the house because sidearms for a man of his rank were only issued on such occasions. As I had yet to pin Erwin down on his closeness to senior officers I asked him if he had ever carried a sidearm. He instantly and affirmatively replied that he hadn't. The *Soldbuch* recorded that he had been issued sidearms on at least two occasions.

He was only granted two periods of leave beyond five days. The first was in 1942 which may well correspond with the photograph of him visiting his injured brother (plate 8). The second in April 1944 which was also to Berlin. It was at this time the last formal photograph of Erwin in unform was taken in Berlin and eventually sent to his father from Normandy shortly before the Allied invasion (front cover).

After my initial trawl of the pages, I contacted both Martina and Kathryn. Kathryn had translated previous documents early on and was again a great help with the *Soldbuch*. One page indicated that Erwin had received three awards, the first his medal for serving on the Eastern Front, the second appears to be one that was awarded when wounded, the *Verwundetenabzeichen*. This almost certainly related to the occasion which Erwin describes in his memoirs, how he and three of his comrades as part of a gun attachment came under fire and took a direct hit. One was killed, one lost an arm, the third badly hurt and Erwin claimed he came out of it unscathed because, 'the Lord had protected' him. If this was the incident then he was sufficiently wounded for him to receive the *Verwundetenabzeichen*. The award was made in March 1943 when the Leibstandarte were fighting in Kharkiv.

The last award was of great interest to me. It was presented on 20 April 1944, Hitler's birthday. On discovering that Martina's mother had lived near the Wolf's Lair, Hitler's Eastern Front Headquarters, Erwin said that he had visited there during the war. This is something he didn't mention to me but on hearing this from Martina after the funeral I did a little research. I found a photograph in Danny Parker's exhaustive biography *Peiper's War*[xxiv] of Peiper presenting Hitler a birthday present from the Leibstandarte at the Wolf's Lair on 27 April 1944. As Erwin confirmed in his final days that he had been Peiper's driver this could well have been the occasion for his visit to the Wolf's Lair. It may well have been then that Erwin met Hitler's driver Erich Kempka and his bodyguard Rochus Misch (mentioned earlier).

When Erwin told Martina many years ago of his membership of the SS he had asked her if this knowledge change her perceptions of him. She replied that it didn't. She shared this with me after we had looked through the *Soldbuch*. I believe Erwin struggled with this throughout his post-war years, probably increasingly so. Which is probably what helped make him the person he became: congenial, and certainly avuncular. I came to understand this as his attempt, in his mind, to make up for those three years and the years leading up to them. My view of Erwin went through many changes, how could it have not? What never changed is my understanding that a human being has no purchase on where or when they are born, and into what circumstances. It is inevitable that we are people of our time and place. Though it is equally so that we change with time, through experience, encounters, and sometimes not a little effort. We can never stay the same but our attitude and behaviour can worsen or improve.

The sight of the *Soldbuch* had taken me back again to a past that I did not belong to but one with which I had grown familiar with over the course of my lifetime. From schoolboy *Commando* books at 1 shilling (5 new pence) a copy in the '60s, through the World at War Series in the '70s, veterans and survivors in the '80s and '90s, and Erwin throughout the first quarter of the 21st century. Books, fiction as well as non-fiction, documentaries and commemorative events, people I have known, witnesses who could tell their stories, survivors who experienced the worst things even now we, we who were not there, cannot fully imagine. All of these had informed me. And now, now a document that spoke of one man's past. Just three years in a life that spanned a century, three years that defined his next eight decades. I began to wonder, as I had done before, yet never so much now as I had then, how my life is defined. What occurred, no matter how brief the period of time, that will never leave me. I thought of how so many of us have an untold experience, a buried past, views we cannot express, the fears we hope will never be realised. I considered how little neighbours actually know of each other. Of how reticent we are to enquire about a person's story. Perhaps that is why ancestry programmes on TV are so popular. We get to know about people from a safe distance. We get to know celebrities, or so we think, better than we know the person next door. So many of us have unknowingly acquired sophisticated exit strategies in conversations, either to avoid disclosing something of ourselves or to avoid hearing something that would annoyingly take up our time. Maybe getting drawn into such a conversation would change our perceptions, especially if that person is different to us with a very different life story. And this is how it began. How could I have known that a brief conversation at a Holocaust Memorial Day event would continue for another 20 years. A conversation that would change my views and my life. A conversation that begs me to urge a lesson upon our world. Namely that we take the time to listen to one another, to engage with whatever they have to teach us from their experiences, and to play a part in preventing this apparently inexorable journey to repeating today the mistakes of the past.

EPILOGUE

No one can determine when and where they are born; into which family or what circumstance. No one can predict how their childhood experiences and environment will impact upon their later years; nor where their early choices will take them.

Because life's anomalies are manifold, a preferred outcome cannot be guaranteed, an aspiration may never be realised, nor a chosen destination arrived at. There are just too many factors at play to determine how a life will proceed and conclude.

The years can often be energised by random acts of generosity and affirmation, but equally so damaged by the cruelty and indifference of others. The wielding of power or falling foul of it may not be entirely within a person's control. To survive against the odds is a driving force within all that walk this earth. If the only choice is kill or be killed, few will opt for the latter.

None of us, therefore, has the right to condemn utterly a person without a comprehensive examination of the facts, nor without an explanation of why they made the choices they did, assuming of course they were at liberty to act on an informed judgement.

No one knows how their life will end, nor when, nor where. It could be late, it could be soon, the scenario changing at any point. It could be because of a haphazard act on the part of another, or an error of judgment, the fault of someone else or one's own.

However, the same fate awaits us all. How we acted, given the specific conditions and context of our time, or if we later responded with remorse to those occasions we did wrong or evaded the chance to be lauded when we did something worthy of praise, will establish whether we lived well.

NOTES

I am grateful to the Bundesarchiv (Federal Archive) for locating Erwin's documents in their possession, especially Frau Irma Martel. These are referred to in the text.

The Soldbuch was located in Tegel - BArch, Federal Archive reference PERS 11 (card index)/Stahlberg, Erwin (03.04.1922).

Personnel Card Bundesarchiv, B 563-1 KARTEI/

Federal Archive reference B 563-1 FILE/S-2315/524)

Clues about what was being sought could be found in the loss report (Federal Archive reference B 563/200056).

In the ZA 11 and 12 Prisoners of War Information Bureau collection, documents about Erwin's captivity were located. These included:

- Personal Particulars dated 8 Dec 1944 (Federal Archive ZA 11/238)
- POW Record including camps (Federal Archive ZA 11/6719)
- POW Form including personal details (Federal Archive ZA 12/81423)

i The *Kindertransport,* (children's transport) was the organized rescue of Jewish children from Germany and Nazi-occupied territories in the year leading up to the Second World War.

ii The *St Louis* was a German transatlantic liner that set sail from Hamburg with 937 passengers, mostly Jews, seeking refuge from the Third Reich. Many had applied for entry to the United States and were going to disembark in Cuba before travelling on to the US. Fewer than 30 were permitted entry at Havanna. Eventually, after the US refused to come to their aid the remaining passengers sailed back across the Atlantic. Britain took in 288, the Netherlands 181, Belgium 214, and 224 found temporary refuge in France.

iii Micheal O'Siadhail, *The Gossamer Wall – Poems in Witness to the Holocaust,* Bloodaxe Books.

iv I was to later discover an anomaly in this account. According to the records in the *Bundesarchiv,* Erwin was not held at the Haverfordwest

PoW Camp which would have billeted prisoners around the St David's peninsula in May 1946. He was held there from 23 October 1945 to 10 January 1946 before being transferred to Llanddarog, Carmarthenshire until 6 July 1947. Perhaps his memory was playing games and that he was confusing his time in and around St David's with another location. Or, maybe, the bonfire was for an occasion other than VE night, perhaps 5 November, which would certainly fit with his time near St David's.

v Erwin would spend four years in eight British PoW camps: 30 November 1944 Green Fields Camp, Ellesmere Road, Shrewsbury; 5 March 1945 Holywood Camp, Belfast; 15 August Dog & Duck Cottage, Norton-in-Malton, Yorkshire; 3 October1945 Happenden Camp, Douglas Castle, South Lanarkshire; 6 October 1945 Comrie Camp, Perthshire; 23 October Haverfordwest, Pembrokeshire; 10 January 1946 Llanddarog Camp, Carmarthenshire; 6 July 1947 Ledbury Camp, Herefordshire. He would be discharged from Ledbury on 20 December 1948.

vi Laura Spinney, *Pale Rider – The Spanish Flu of 1918 and How it Changed the World*, Jonathan Cape, 2017.

vii Erich Kern, *Dance of Death*, Collins, 1951, p.76.

viii ibid, p.60.

ix Erwin Bartmann, *Für Volk and Führer*, Helion & Company 2013, p.218.

x ibid p.224.

xi Werner Kindler, *Obedient Unto Death*, Frontline Books 2014.

xii Herbert Maeger, *Lost Honour, Betrayed Loyalty*, Frontline Books 2015.

xiii ibid p.61.

xiv Jens Westermeier, *Joachim Peiper, A Biography of Himler's SS Commander*, Schiffer Military History, 2007.

xv Grossman, Vasily, *Life and Fate*, Vintage 2006, p.143.

xvi Bartmann, op. cit., p.92.

xvii Westemeier, op. cit., p.16.

xviii Bruce D. Thompson, *Echoes of Contempt, A History of Judeophobia and the Christian Church*, Wipf & Stock, 2018.

xix Parker, Danny S. (2014). *Hitler's Warrior: The Life and Wars of SS Colonel Jochen Peiper*. Da Capo Press, pp.95-96.

xx Maeger, ibid, p.48f.

xxi Rudolf Lehmann, *Die Leibstandarte Im Bild*, Lehmann 2001, p.266.

xxii Statement by the Right Reverend Bishop Otto Melle at the World Church Conference in Oxford on 22 July 1937, transcript Imperial War Museum, London.

xxiii E. Amy Buller, *Darkness Over German, a warning from history*, Arcadia Books 2017, p.38, originally published by Longmans, Green, and Co 1943.

xxiv Danny S. Parker, *Peiper's War, The Wartime Years of SS Leader Jochen Peiper 1941-44*, Frontline Books 2019.

BIBLIOGRAPHY

Background to Nazi Germany

Bielenberg, Christabel, *The Past is Myself,* Chatto & Windus, 1968.

Buller, E. Amy, *Darkness over Germany, a Warning from History,* Arcadia Books, 2017 (orig. pub. Longmans, Green and Co, 1943). NB This is a record of conversations held by Buller, an English academic, with members of German Society leading up to the war.

Fulbrook, Mary, *A Small Town Near Auschwitz,* Oxford University Press, 2012.

Knopp, Guido, *Hitler's Children,* English translation pub. Sutton Publishing, 2002 (orig. pub. C. Bertlesmann, Munich, 2000).

Krug, Nora, Heimat, *A German Family Album,* Particular Books, 2018. [NB a highly visual account of a second-generation German after the end of the Second World War exploring her family's past].

Vassiltchikov, Marie, *The Berlin Diaries,* Chatto & Windus Ltd., 1985.

Background to Antisemitism

Ericksen, Robert P., *Complicity in the Holocaust, Churches and Universities in Nazi Germany,* Cambridge University Press, 2012.

Graml, Hermann, *Antisemitism in the Third Reich,* Blackwell Publishers, 1992.

Nirenberg, David, *Anti-Judaism, The Western Tradition,* Norton, 2013.

Steigmann-Gall, Richard, *The Holy Reich, Nazi Conceptions of Christianity 1919-1945,* Cambridge University Press, 2003.

Thompson, Bruce D., *Echoes of Contempt, A History of Judeophobia and the Christian Church,* Wipf & Stock, 2018.

Novels on pre-war and wartime Germany

Boll, Heinrich, *The Train Was On Time,* Penguin Random House UK, 2019 (orig. pub. in Germany in 1949). [NB This has a comprehensive description of what it was like to travel on a troop train to the Eastern Front, as did Erwin.]

Boschwitz, Ulrich Alexander, *The Passenger,* Pushkin Press, 2021 (orig. pub. in Germany, 2018).

Fallada, Hans, *Little Man What Now,* Putnam, 1933, (orig. pub. in Germany, 1932).

Gerlach, *Breakout at Stalingrad,* Apolo 2018 (orig. pub. by Kiepenhheur & Witsch 2016). [NB A remarkable first-hand account of the Stalingrad Pocket from a German perspective.]

Keilson, Hans, *The Death of the Adversary,* Vintage, 2011 (orig. pub. in German in 1959).

Kempowski, Walter, *All for Nothing,* Granta Publications, 2015 (orig. pub. Albrecht Knaus Verlag, Munich 2006).

Lampe, Friedo, *At the Edge of Night,* Hesperus Press Limited, 2019 (orig. pub. in German in 1933).

The Holocaust

Cesarani, David, *Final Solution, The Fate of the Jews 1933-49,* Macmillan, 2016.

Friedlander Saul, *The Years of Extermination, Nazi Germany and the Jews 1939-1945,* Wiedenfeld & Nicolson, 2007.

Longerich, Peter, *Holocaust, The Nazi Persecution and Murder of the Jews,* Oxford University Press, 2010.

Schloss, Eva, *After Auschwitz, A Story of Heartbreak and Survival by the Stepsister of Anne Frank,* Hodder & Stoughton, 2013.

Snyder, Timothy, *Black Earth, The Holocaust as History and Warning,* Tim Duggan Books, 2015.

Zabarko, Boris (Ed.), *Holocaust in the Ukraine,* Vallentine Mitchell & Co Ltd, 2005. (NB A collection of reflections representative of the suffering of Jewish Ukrainians).

Books on the SS Leibstandarte Adolf Hitler

Butler, Rupert, *SS Leibstandarte, The History of the First SS Division, 1933-45,* Amber Books, 2015.

Parker, Danny S., *Peiper's War, The Wartime Years of SS Leader Jochen Peiper 1941-44,* Frontline Books, 2019.

Pontolillo, James, *Murderous Elite, The Waffen-SS and its complete record of war crimes,* Leandoer & Ekholm Publishing, Stockholm, 2009.

Villani, Gerry, *Voices of the Waffen SS,* Gerry Villani, 2015.

Westemeier, Jens, Joachim Peiper, *A Biography of Himmler's SS Commander,* Schiffer Publishing, 2007.

[NB Taylor, Brian, *Barbarossa to Berlin, a Chronology of the Campaigns on the Eastern Front 1941-1945,* Vols 1 & 2, Spellmount Limited, 2003 and 2004 respectively]

Memoirs

Bartmann, Erwin, Für Volk and Führer, *The Memoir of a Veteran of the 1st SS Panzer Division Leibstandarte SS Adolf Hitler,* Helion & Company, 2013

Kempka, Erich, *I was Hitler's Chauffeur,* Frontline Books, 2012 (orig. pub. Kryburg, Munich, 1951)

Kern, Eric, *Dance of Death,* Collins, 1951 (orig. pub. By Thomas Verlag, Zurich, 1948)

Kindler, Werner, *Obedient Unto Death, A Panzer Grenadier of the Leibstandarte-SS Adolf Hitler,* Frontline Books, 2010 (orig. pub. Werner Kindler 2010)

Maeger, Herbert, *Lost Honour, Betrayed Loyalty, the Memoir of a Waffen-SS Soldier on the Eastern Front,* Frontline Books, 2015. (orig. pub. Rosenheimer Verlagshaus, 2002)

Misch, Rochus, *Hitler's Last Witness, The Memoirs of Hitler's Bodyguard,* Frontline Books, 2014.

[NB David Park, *Spies in Canaan,* Bloomsbury Publishing, 2022. Within the novel is an account of a conversation between a man and his older ex line manager. The former is having to consider whether it right to seek information from the latter about his past, in this instance the Vietnam War. The epigraph at the beginning of *No Ordinary Neighbour* is a quote from *Spies in Canaan.*]

INDEX